Reading
Without
Nonsense

Other books by Frank Smith:

The Genesis of Language: A Psycholinguistic Approach
(edited, with George A. Miller) (1966)

Psycholinguistics and Reading (1973)

*Comprehension and Learning: A Conceptual Framework
for Teachers* (1975)

Understanding Reading, Third Edition (1982)

Writing and the Writer (1982)

*Essays Into Literacy: Selected Papers and Some
Afterthoughts* (1983)

Awakening to Literacy (edited, with Hillel Goelman
and Antoinette A. Oberg) (1984)

Reading
Without
Nonsense

FRANK SMITH

Teachers College, Columbia University
New York and London

Published by Teachers College Press, 1234 Amsterdam Avenue, New York, N.Y. 10027

First edition published in 1978 in England by Cambridge University Press under the title *Reading,* and in 1979 in the United States by Teachers College Press under the title *Reading Without Nonsense.* Copyright © 1978 by Frank Smith.

Library of Congress Cataloging in Publication Data

Smith, Frank, 1928–
  Reading without nonsense.

  Originally published under title: Reading. Cambridge:
Cambridge University Press, c1978.
  Bibliography: p.
  Includes index.
  1. Reading.   I. Title.
LB1050.S5732   1985   428.4   85-2694
ISBN 0-8077-2768-7

Manufactured in the United States of America

90 89 88 87 86 85   2 3 4 5 6

Contents

Preface
to the Second Edition

In the first edition of this book, I described the ease with which children become literate when they are personally involved with people actually making use of the signs, labels, lists, newspapers, magazines, and books in the world around them. In contrast, I examined the difficulty many children experience with formal reading instruction based on exercises, material, and drills that are to a large extent nonsensical. The philosophy of this kind of instruction, which I now call "programmatic," is that reading is a set of skills that can be taught and mastered in a predetermined sequence, provided there is a closely managed "systems" approach with properly specified objectives and frequent tests. Programmatic instruction is the antithesis of meaningful language experience for teachers and children. It is primarily a method of control.

Since the first edition was published in 1978 the issues have become more clearly demarcated and the conflict more acute. On the one hand, the programmatic approach to reading instruction has clearly failed. No one claims that children are reading better today than they were ten years ago, or even than they were 25 years ago, when the development of rigorously controlled instructional programs for literacy education began to proliferate. That was the time when many influential educational leaders thought that the technology that would put man on the moon would also be a certain cure for illiteracy. One might think that most politicians and administrators by now would have recognized that the "remedy" for illiteracy might instead be a contributing factor. But with the failure has come a clamor for even more programs, for even tighter control of schools and teachers in the name of "accountability." All this may sound reasonable but it constrains teachers to teach in the manner decreed by outside authorities who know nothing of the particular children in their classroom, of their unique individual interests, concerns, and difficulties. Teachers are expected to conform to the program, no matter how trivial, misconceived, and ultimately damaging to literacy the instruction might be. If the bleeding treatment does not seem to be restoring the patient to life, bleed some more.

On the other hand, extensive research in many cultures has confirmed what many experienced teachers have known intuitively: that children become readers when they are engaged in situations where written language is being meaningfully used, much the way they learn spoken language from their association with people around them who use speech in meaningful ways. This is the opposite of programmatic instruction. The implications of this research have been slow to break through at decision-making levels of education, primarily because they would replace stringent outside control of classroom activity with trust that teachers can teach and that children will learn if both are given reasonable autonomy.

As the theoretical issues and conceptual differences have become more clearly defined, the conflict itself has become more acute. A new technological factor has speeded up the time scale and exacerbated the threat. I am referring to the computer, the ultimate programmatic instructional device. People who like programmatic instruction love computers, because they promise to teach all the exercises and drills more efficiently than teachers at a much lower cost. Used in this way, computers could destroy both literacy and the teaching profession.

Most of what I said in the first edition about children, learning, and language remains unchanged. The nature of all of these remains the same, despite technological developments. We may endeavor to teach children differently, but their brains learn as they always did. Language is changing only in its most superficial aspects, and it is always developing in that way. Where recent research has led me to revise what I said about children, learning, or language in the first edition of this book, it has generally been to provide new evidence or observations in support of particular points.

A significant addition to this second edition is recent material on early literacy, enabling me to expand the topic of learning to read into a new chapter in its own right. I have also added a closing chapter on the promise and threat of computers in literacy education.

Preface
to the First Edition

It is not difficult to make reading impossible.

I am not referring to such obvious disruptions as distracting the reader's attention, tearing out pages, defacing the print, switching off the lights, or even making the reading material a book written in a dull and incomprehensible manner, although a book that does not make sense will certainly be difficult to read.

I mean that it is easy to make a book unreadable for a person who otherwise would be able to pick up that same book and read it fluently. One very effective way to produce incomprehensibility is to ensure that the person trying to read the book is apprehensive about making a mistake, for example while reading aloud. Reading is not easily accomplished if you are nervous about your performance. Equally handicapping can be the endeavor to memorize every trivial detail in order to avoid being caught out in a subsequent cross-examination or written exercise, especially if the exercise is to be graded and the evaluation to become part of a permanent record that perhaps could make a difference to a career. Anxiety and the indiscriminate effort to achieve total recall both help to explain the widely experienced phenomenon of textbooks that are nonsense before an examination yet transparently comprehensible after.

If my catalog of obstacles to reading comprehension sounds suspiciously like a description of the circumstances in which many students find themselves in school, the coincidence is entirely intentional. Just as it is not difficult to make a book unreadable, so it is easy to make learning to read impossible. Even when there is a sincere intention to help children to read, the instruction can beset them with handicaps guaranteed to interfere with learning. Bad habits can be taught so effectively that whatever an individual tries to read in later life will be found incomprehensible.

This book is primarily concerned with the process of reading, with the perceptual and language skills involved in reading and with the nature of the task confronting children attempting to learn to read. But the implications of the book are instructional. I shall try to show why it is that it is only through reading that children learn to read, and that a teacher's role must therefore be to make reading easy for every child. In particular I shall argue that children can learn to read only through materials and activities that make sense to them, that they can relate to what they already know or want to know. Anything that children cannot relate to what they already know will be nonsense to them, whether or not it is nonsense to the teacher. Expecting children to learn to read through nonsense is the easiest method of making learning to read impossible—and unfortunately the most widespread.

This book is addressed to anyone interested or involved in the topic of reading—primarily to teachers and to students and faculty in colleges of education, although it should also be relevant to parents and to others who perhaps may be concerned about their own reading ability. How can one book be directed to such a varied audience? By focusing on the nature of reading, rather than asserting a particular point of view about reading instruction. This book contains no easy message about how reading might be taught or improved at any age level; in fact I argue that the solution to "reading problems" cannot lie in any particular reading methodology or set of reading materials. The only practical educational conclusion that can be drawn from an analysis of the relatively few fundamental ideas that have come, gone, and continually returned throughout over twenty centuries of reading instruction—always with the result that some children have learned to read but others have failed—is that the universal concern should change from what teachers should *do* to what teachers should *know*.

Teacher training institutions seem often to expect teachers of reading to do their jobs without a basic understanding of the topic they are concerned with—and teachers frequently achieve remarkable success under such conditions. Education would be in a far sorrier state today were it not for teachers' untutored intuitions and insights. But as far as their own formal education is concerned, most teachers are left with a patchwork of conflicting practical suggestions and a belief that the nature of reading is either too obvious to require analysis or too mysterious to be discussed.

Yet the nature of reading cannot be ignored since the success of reading instruction must ultimately depend on whether the instruction makes reading easy or difficult. And in order to understand whether a particular method or set of materials will make reading easy or difficult, whether they will make sense or nonsense to a child, there is no alternative to acquiring an understanding of reading itself.

The purpose of this book is to contribute to such an understanding of reading. The orientation is *scientific;* the assertions that I make about language and the brain are based on scientific evidence. But I have not overburdened the text with detailed references, footnotes, or theoretical debate. My aim is readability; the technical discussions and supporting arguments can be found in my more specialized book *Understanding Reading,* Third Edition (New York: Holt, Rinehart and Winston, 1982). My emphasis, as I have indicated, is on the importance of sense. Nothing can be taught unless it has the potential of making sense to the learner, and learning itself is nothing but the endeavor to make sense. The effort to teach or to inform, therefore, can be nothing but an endeavor to make sense, to be comprehensible. I hope indeed that this book will make sense to everyone concerned with literacy.

Reading
Without
Nonsense

1

Making Sense of Reading

A preliminary glance through these pages might indicate that despite its title this book contains very little that is specifically on the topic of reading. But the first point to be stressed is that there is nothing about reading that is unique. In order to make sense of what takes place when we read, a number of more general topics must be explored.

Reading and the Brain

There is nothing about reading that is unique, whether one considers the structure or the functions of the brain. Despite the diagrams that sometimes appear in textbooks allocating specific responsibilities to different locations on the surface of the brain, reading is not the exclusive concern of any one particular part. Anatomists and physiologists have not isolated a specialized "reading center" in the brain. Many areas of the brain are active when we read, but none are involved with reading to the exclusion of anything else. Illness or injury may occasionally affect the working of the brain so that ability to read is disturbed, but almost certainly some more general activity involving either language or vision will also be impaired.

There is also nothing about reading that is unique as far as intellectual processes are concerned. From the point of view of language, reading makes no demands that the brain does not meet in the comprehension of speech. And visually there is nothing in reading that the eyes and brain do not accomplish when we look around a room to locate an object or to distinguish one face from another.

Researchers are discovering that in order to understand reading they must consider not just the eyes but also the mechanisms of memory and attention, anxiety, risk taking, the nature and uses of language, the comprehension of speech, interpersonal relations, sociocultural differences, learning in general, and the learning of young children in particular. All these are topics that we shall be concerned with in this book, at least to the extent that they are relevant to reading.

Fortunately there is a good deal in all these topics that is interesting in its own right. Fortunately also, when all these topics have been examined for the light they shed on reading, there is very little about reading itself that is left to be said. It is rather like climbing some hills; not until you reach the top do you get the best view of where you have been. When you have covered all the ground, not only have you gained insight into reading, but you also know a good deal about many other aspects of the human intellect, especially with respect to learning. Teachers in other areas find that such an analysis of reading also gives them a deeper understanding of the problems of comprehending subjects like science, music, or mathematics.

Reading and Instruction

Examination of a wide range of topics relevant to reading not only leaves little to be said about reading itself, it leaves little to be added about how reading should be taught. Instructional implications become self-evident. The more closely one delves into the nature of reading, the less one tends or needs to be dogmatic about what teachers ought to do in classrooms. Such an open-minded attitude toward instruction runs counter to the majority of books about reading, and indeed to much of the research that has been carried out on reading. Partly because reading is a complex topic, but mainly I think because it is so widely regarded as a compelling educational problem, priority in most studies of reading is usually given to what might be done to improve instruction rather than to understanding the process in the first place.

As I suggested in the preface, the training of teachers often seems to assume that the problem *is* instruction—that teachers should be told what they should do rather than what they should know. The training of teachers does not invariably encourage them to make their own decisions. Even books that purport to be concerned with the psychology or process of reading tend to be heavily weighted in favor of some particular theory about how reading should be taught. The authors are perhaps not entirely to blame. Often they are or have been practising teachers who rarely have had the opportunity in the classroom to separate what they do from why they do it. But even "experts" from outside fields (like psychology or linguistics) who write about what they think is relevant to reading are likely to be held responsible for translating their conclusions directly into practice. The belief that it is not enough to *inform* teachers—that they should be *instructed*—dies hard, even among teachers themselves.

To argue that questions like "What is the best way to teach

reading?'' are too simplistic is likely to provoke the ultimate challenge: "Don't beat around the bush. Tell me what *you* would do if *you* had to face thirty-five kids in a reading class on Monday morning?'' This is rather like asking for a straight answer to the simple question of how far nails should be driven into wood. The only reasonable response to such a blanket question is rather impolite: "If I were really responsible for teaching reading to thirty-five children on Monday morning, I would make sure I knew enough about reading in general and about those children in particular that I would never have to ask an outsider such a question.''

Besides, the teacher's problem is never the absence of advice. The world is full of experts willing to promote a favorite remedy for reading problems. But if one authority says Method A is best and a second prefers Method B, how can a third opinion possibly help make up the teacher's mind? The teacher does not need advice, but understanding. The teacher still has to make the decision.

And there is no point in expecting research to resolve the dilemma. Hundreds of methods of teaching reading exist, mostly minor variations on a few traditional themes, and literally tens of thousands of research studies have been done comparing one method or procedure or set of materials with another. And out of these tens of thousands of studies only one basic and incontrovertible conclusion can be drawn: *all methods of teaching reading can achieve some success, with some children, some of the time.*

In the two-thousand-year recorded history of reading instruction, as far as I have been able to discover, no one has devised a method of teaching reading that has proved totally fruitless. No matter how bizarre an approach might seem to be, research studies can always be found claiming not only that it succeeded in teaching something, but also that it did so relatively better than some other method. All this research seems to prove just one thing—that children are incredibly flexible and resilient. Children seem able to learn to read *despite* the method of instruction that is employed. At this point, credit must be given to teachers (who too often are held responsible only for the failures). Many teachers seem able to teach children to read, no matter what method they employ, although others, with some children at least, may follow exactly the same procedures in vain. In any case, the better teachers are always intelligently eclectic; they use what works when they see that it can work, even though they may not be sure why.

Unhappily, although every method of reading instruction seems to achieve some success with some children, no method succeeds with all children. As we shall see, all methods of teaching reading must exact a price from the child attempting to learn, and in some circumstances, therefore, all methods can interfere with reading. So once again, what the teacher needs is an understanding of the particular possibilities and costs (to the child) of different methods and materials, an understanding of the particular children and what they are finding easy and difficult, and an understanding of reading and how children must learn to read. Without such understanding, teachers cannot make up their own minds about methods and materials, and are forced to fall back on the exhortations of experts or the blandishments of publishers. Such teachers must work without knowing why they succeed or fail. Without understanding, instruction is founded on superstition.

The teacher's dilemma in the selection of instructional techniques is also not likely to be resolved by the discovery of a new and ideal method for teaching all children. From the huge expenditures of commercial enterprises and government agencies in pursuit of a technology of reading instruction that will prove infallible, and preferably "teacher-proof," the only conclusion that can safely be drawn is that nothing could possibly be invented that is significantly better than or even different from the methods and materials we have always had available, even if they are dressed up for use with computers. Children have been learning to read for centuries without the benefit of technology. We need to discover only what we have been doing wrong—and doing right—in the past. Many people reading this book developed their skill in stuffy, badly lit, and overcrowded classrooms, with desks nailed in rows to the floor, using ill-printed and sanctimonious materials in an authoritarian atmosphere that would rarely be tolerated today. Today's children are not that much different from the children we were, and we learned to read without the advantages of systems research, behaviorally defined objectives, or teacher accountability. The "systems approach" involves breaking down reading into "component skills"—and I propose to argue that "breaking down reading" makes learning to read more difficult because it makes nonsense out of what should be sense. To learn to read, children need to be helped to read. The issue is as simple and as difficult as that.

Two basic necessities for learning to read are the availability of interesting material that makes sense to the learner and an understanding and more experienced reader as a guide. As far as materials are concerned, the problem is one of surfeit rather than scarcity. We are inundated with books, magazines, newspapers, comics, television commercials, computer display terminals, street signs, brand names, notices, billboards, handouts, instruction manuals, menus, timetables, labels, and wrappers, not to mention blank paper and a host of other writing surfaces ranging from walls to T-shirts and a variety of marking instruments. The teacher's dilemma is again not so much to find as to select. I am not so sure about the supply of understanding adults. Certainly there are many well-motivated people—one in every classroom, I would trust. But whether they all have sufficient understanding, either about how children learn or what is involved in reading, is another matter.

There is one final reason why blind faith in methods or materials will not solve problems of instruction in reading, a reason that will require the remainder of this book to explain. The final reason is this: *children cannot be taught to read.* A teacher's responsibility is not to teach children to read but to make it possible for them to learn to read. There is a difference. I want to show in this book that the real skills of reading, which have made readers out of you and me, are not skills that are formally taught at school or ever could be. We have acquired these skills only through the practice of reading. Most of the time we are not even aware of what these skills are, and they are certainly not explained in the majority of teacher-training institutions.

Learning to Read

I have said that there is nothing unique about reading physiologically, visually, or linguistically; these are assertions that will be justified in the course of this book. I shall also try to show that there is nothing unique about learning to read. No special, exotic, or particularly difficult learning skills are required. Learning to read involves no learning ability that children have not already exercised in order to understand the language spoken at home or to make sense of the visual world around them. In fact, learning to read should be very much simpler, given the complexity of these earlier language and visual accomplishments.

Adults often underrate the intellectual achievements of very young children in mastering language or learning to use their eyes. This belittling of the innate capacity of children to learn is largely based on the unwarranted assumption that anything that is not specifically taught cannot involve much learning. Another aim in this book is to demonstrate the tremendous intellectual achievements of children during the first few years of their lives, and especially during the first few months, not only without formal instruction but at a time when adults rarely suspect that any significant learning is taking place. We learn so efficiently as infants that by the time we are old enough to appreciate our achievements, our skills have become as effortless as breathing.

Perhaps one example might be in order. We take it for granted that all infants know or soon recognize that they have only one mother. We rarely consider that babies might be confused about the person who appears at one time in a red dress and another time in a blue trouser suit, or that the mother in the bedroom may not be regarded as the same mother in the bathroom or in the kitchen. Adults take all this for granted because they *know* that these different manifestations are all of the same person. But how do infants learn this? Where do they acquire the information?

For the first few months of their lives, children do not realize that they have only one mother. For infants the mother in the bedroom is not the same as the mother in the bathroom or the mother in the kitchen. This peculiarity of an infant's perception of his world was discovered by an ingenious researcher who contrived to present babies with more than one mother at a time. The experimental procedure was not complicated; he simply confronted infants with three mothers simultaneously: the real one and two reflections in mirrors. Babies who suddenly saw three mothers at one time scarcely paused from sucking their bottles. The response seemed to be, "So you've all got together for once"—provided the babies were less than about five months of age. But when infants older than five months were confronted by triplicate mothers there was a difference. They stopped sucking at their bottles, their pupils dilated, their heart rate increased, and their breathing accelerated. They were interested, they were surprised, they were seeing something they did not expect. At about the fifth month of their lives, they had decided—obviously without instruction—that while some identical objects might be endlessly duplicated, like the spoon in the bathroom and the spoon in the kitchen, a few objects frequently change appearance yet remain unique. This is not an inconsiderable learning achievement, but it is accomplished so effortlessly that when we are older it is difficult to realize that a problem existed in the first place.

Children spend the first years of life solving problems all the time. Probably more learning takes place in the first two years than in any similar period thereafter. Children are born learning; if there is nothing to learn they are bored and their attention is distracted. We do not have to train children to learn, or even account for their learning; we have to avoid interfering with it.

Let me be more specific. Children who have learned to comprehend spoken language (not necessarily the language of school, but
some language that makes sense in the world they live in) and who can
see sufficiently well to distinguish a pin from a paper clip on the table in
front of them have already demonstrated sufficient language, visual
acuity, and learning ability to learn how to read. Learning to read is
easy for a child—or should be, were it not for the fact that it is easy for
adults, even well-intentioned ones, to make learning to read difficult.

However, the fact that there is nothing unique about reading or
learning to read does not mean that children who learn with facility in
every other respect may never experience difficulty in reading. We all
know that is not the case. But a child who can see and can comprehend
speech cannot be a failure at reading because of a "specific learning
disability," or minimal brain dysfunction, or dyslexia, or any of the
other terms that are used to conceal ignorance about why some
children fail to learn to read. As I have said, there is no structure or
function in the brain that is exclusive to reading. Nor can such a child
fail because of a lack of intelligence. Indeed, children do not need to be
very smart to learn to read (although learning to read will certainly
help make them smarter). Children will fail to learn to read who do not
want to read, who cannot make sense of it, or who find the price of
learning too high. They will fail if they get the wrong idea of what
reading is. Children are constantly learning, and teaching can sometimes have unplanned outcomes. A child may learn not to want to read,
or not to expect to be able to read, or may even learn to approach
reading in ways that will have the effect of always making it difficult or
impossible.

Reading cannot be taught, but teachers and other adults nonethe-
less have a critical role to play and bear great responsibility in making
learning to read possible for a child.

Preview

In Chapter 2 I shall look at vision and show that there is nothing
unique that the eyes and brain have to do in reading. But I shall go
further and show that skill in reading actually depends on using the
eyes as little as possible, that as we become fluent readers we learn to
rely more on what we already know, on what is behind the eyeballs,
and less on the print on the page in front of us. Paradoxically, the more
we look the less we are likely to see. Too much emphasis on the eyes in
reading can make you functionally blind—and that is the situation in

which many children with normal vision may find themselves when they try to make sense of reading instruction.

Chapter 3 is concerned with memory, and explains another paradox whereby the more we try to memorize as we read, the less we are likely to comprehend and remember. Another of the critical but untaught skills of reading is to make the maximum use of what we already know and to be as economical as possible in putting new information into memory.

In Chapter 4 I look at language, and in particular the nature of meaning. I shall explain that meaning is not something that a reader or listener *gets from* language, but something that is brought to language. The difference is important, for it demonstrates that reading is not a passive activity but involves complex intellectual processes that must always be actively initiated and directed by the reader. Other important points in this chapter are that reading is not "decoding to sound" and that children cannot learn to read by memorizing phonic rules.

Chapter 5 is concerned with comprehension and learning and develops the theme of Chapter 4 that reading is an active process. Readers are not passive recipients of meaning from print, but must predict if they are to comprehend. But such prediction is not a special or difficult activity exclusive to language comprehension. Rather it is one of those unsuspected skills we have been exercising all our lives, and is the basis of learning.

Chapter 6 gets to the heart of reading, analyzing the skills that a fluent reader must possess and the insights that children must achieve in order to learn to read.

In Chapter 7 the focus is directly upon children, examining the ways in which they solve—or may fail to solve—the riddles of learning to read. Children need to be admitted into the "literacy club," where they can see written language in use and can find help in using it themselves.

By Chapter 8 I shall be ready at last to look at reading from the teacher's point of view, summarizing those factors that determine whether learning to read will be easy or difficult for a child. A number of more specialized topics will be mentioned briefly—dyslexia, learning disability, remedial reading, readiness, dialect differences, and spelling.

Computers will not change the way children learn, but they are changing the way they are taught. Chapter 9 considers ways in which computers can help or hinder children in the process of becoming readers, and also how computers might expand or undermine the teacher's role.

Two Words of Advice

This book is intended to be practical, despite its range over a variety of theoretical disciplines. So perhaps I might conclude this first chapter with a couple of practical hints for the reader concerning the rest of the book.

First, relax. Anxiety about being able to comprehend and remember can make any reader functionally blind. You may not realize that anxiety has this effect, but the more you are concerned about reading this book the less you are likely to comprehend it. Try to *enjoy* the book, put it aside for a while if you are bored or confused, and leave your brain to take care of the rest.

My second helpful hint is that you should not try to memorize anything you read in this book. The effort to memorize is completely destructive of comprehension. On the other hand, with comprehension the memorization will take care of itself. Your brain has had longer experience than you can recall in making sense of a complex world and in remembering what is important.

My two words of advice are exemplified in what I call the Russian Novel Phenomenon. Every reader must have experienced that depressing moment about fifty pages into a Russian novel when we realize that we have lost track of all the characters, the variety of names by which they are known, their family relationships, and relative ranks in the civil service. At this point we can give in to our anxiety, and start again to read more carefully, trying to memorize all the details on the off chance that some may prove to be important. If such a course is followed, the second reading is almost certain to be more incomprehensible than the first. The probable result: one Russian novel lost forever. But there is another alternative: to read faster, to push ahead, to make sense of what we can, and to enjoy whatever we make sense of. And suddenly the book becomes readable, the story makes sense, and we find that we can remember all the important characters and events simply because we now *know* what is important. Any rereading we then have to do is bound to make sense, because at least we comprehend what is going on and what we are looking for.

Summary

Nothing about reading is unique. Reading makes no demands on the eyes that are not met when we look around a room. Reading requires no linguistic ability that is not demonstrated in the understanding of speech. In particular, learning to read involves no special learning skills. Children are highly skilled and experienced learners, although it is possible for them to be confused by reading instruction. Written language must be made meaningful and useful to children who are striving to learn. This essential assistance can be provided by teachers who understand the nature of reading and who know the individual learner, but not by formal programs where instructional decisions are made in advance by someone outside the classroom.

2

Reading—From Behind the Eyes

One essential skill of reading that no reader is ever taught is to depend upon the eyes as little as possible.

Does my opening statement sound absurd? I shall demonstrate that the eyes must play a relatively minor role in reading, and that undue concern with the printed marks on a page serves only to make reading more difficult. It is a basic principle of vision that the more you expect the eyes to do, the less you are likely to see. This principle applies especially in reading, where too much attention to the page in front of you can have the temporary effect of making you functionally blind. The page literally becomes blank. One of the handicaps besetting children learning to read is that often they cannot see more than a few letters at a time. When a teacher calls a child's attention to some words in a book by saying, "There they are in front of your nose. You can see them, can't you?" it may well be that the teacher can see the words but the child cannot. This impediment has nothing to do with children's eyes, but reflects difficulty they are having trying to read. In fact it is easy to put the teacher in the same visual state as the child—by making reading equally difficult for the teacher.

Visual and Nonvisual Information

Of course, the eyes have a part to play in reading. You cannot read with your eyes closed (except for Braille, which is not being considered in this book), or in the dark, or if you have no printed material in front of your eyes. It is necessary for some information from print to reach your brain. Let us call this *visual information,* which obviously must be picked up by the eyes.

But visual information is not enough for reading. I could allow you all the visual information anyone could expect in order to read, yet still

13

you might be unable to do so. For example, I could ask you to read the following passage, which happens to be in Dutch. Unless you understand Dutch, there is no way you will be able to read it:

> Tenslotte is de doorvoer—of transitohandel van groot belang geworden. Nederland ligt tussen drie belangrijke industrie- en mijngebieden.

But possibly you do understand Dutch. I could still confront you with a passage of Dutch or English text that perhaps you could not read:

> Increasing numbers of late Pleistocene macrofossil indicate that boreal spruce forest similar to the existing taiga in Canada was present on the northern Plains at the same time.

And finally, even if I present you with some text in a familiar language on a topic that you fully understand, it still might not be possible for you to read. For example, it could be that you have not learned *how* to read.

I hope you will agree that in the three situations I have just described, it would not be lack of visual information that prevents you from reading. There are some other kinds of information that you also need, including an understanding of the relevant language, familiarity with the subject matter, and some general ability in reading. All these other kinds of information can be lumped together and called *nonvisual information*. It is easy to distinguish visual from nonvisual information. Visual information disappears when the lights go out, nonvisual information is in your head already, behind the eyes. And since both visual and nonvisual information are required for reading, their joint necessity can be represented as in Diagram 1.

Trading Two Kinds of Information

It might appear that I have gone to great pains to state the obvious, that you must already have certain kinds of information in your head in order to read. But there is a relationship between visual and nonvisual information that is not so obvious but of critical importance in reading. The relationship is this: The two kinds of information can be traded-off against each other. There is a reciprocal relationship between the two that might be represented as in Diagram 2 and put formally into words:

The more nonvisual information you have when you read, the less visual information you need.

The less nonvisual information you have when you read, the more visual information you need.

Diagram 1

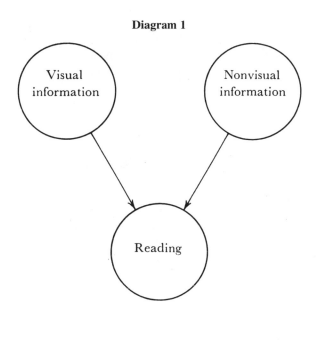

Diagram 2

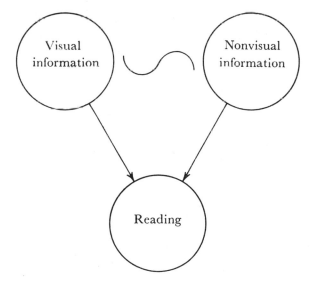

Expressed more colloquially, the more you know already, the less you need to find out. It is as if there is a certain total amount of information required to read anything (the actual amount depending on your purpose and what you are trying to read) and contributions to that total amount can come from in front of the eyes or behind.

It is easy to provide everyday illustrations of the trade-off between the two kinds of information. The more you know in advance about a book, the easier it is to read. You can read an easy book faster, you can read it in smaller print, and you can read it in a relatively poor light. A book that is difficult to read, on the other hand, requires more time, better lighting, and far more considerate printing. The eyes have more work to do if the book is difficult; often you need to peer. In the same way, it is easy to recognize billboards and highway signs from a distance when you know what the words might be, but if you have no idea, or the words are in an unfamiliar language, you have to get closer to distinguish even a single letter. This is not an uncommon phenomenon; the better you are acquainted with a person, or a kind of car or bird or tree, the easier it is to recognize them at a distance.

The fact that visual and nonvisual information can to some extent be substituted for each other is crucial for the following reason: *There is a severe limit to how much visual information the brain can handle.* The eyes can be relieved of strain in reading under less-than-ideal conditions if the reader can bring a lot of nonvisual information or prior knowledge to bear. But it is not the case that a reader can simply slow down and assimilate more visual information whenever the reading gets difficult, because there is a bottleneck between the eyes and the brain, as Diagram 3 indicates. The brain can very easily become overwhelmed by visual information, in which case the ability to see will be limited and may even cease for a while. It is therefore a basic skill of reading—a skill that can be acquired only through reading—to make maximum use of what you know already and to depend on the information from the eyes as little as possible. To explain this phenomenon further, I must digress for a while to make some statements about the nature of seeing in general.

Limitations Upon Seeing

We normally assume that we can see everything that is present in front of our eyes, provided of course that we have our eyes open. It is also our common belief that vision is instantaneous, that we perceive events the moment they occur and see scenes the instant we turn our

Diagram 3

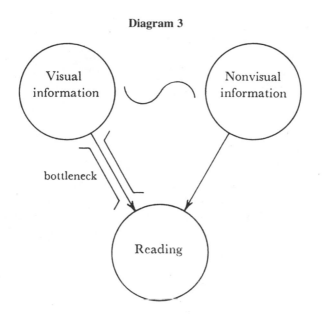

eyes upon them. And we certainly tend to think that it is the eyes themselves that are responsible for what we see. But in fact the eyes do not *see* at all, their sole function is to pick up visual information in the form of light rays and convert it into bursts of nervous energy that travel along the million or so fibers of the optic nerve into the brain. What we see is the brain's interpretation of this barrage of neural impulses. It is the brain that sees, the eyes merely *look*, usually under the direction of the brain. And the brain certainly does not see everything that occurs in front of the eyes. Sometimes, as everyone knows, the brain can make a mistake, in which case we can see something that is not in front of the eyes.

Visual perception, in other words, involves decisions on the part of the brain. If you see a horse across a field, it is because the brain has decided that what you are looking at is a horse. And you will see a horse even if the brain has made a mistake and further consideration leads it to decide and therefore see that you are looking at a cow. If I write an address for you:

210   LION   STREET

what you see is a number, 210, and a couple of words, Lion Street. But if you check back you will see that I wrote the figures 1 and 0 in the number in exactly the same way that I wrote the letters I and O in Lion. The visual information was the same. Whether you saw figures or letters depended on what your brain decided you were looking at.

Not only does seeing require the brain to make decisions, but it takes the brain time to make these decisions. More precisely, the brain uses information—visual information—to make decisions, and the "processing" of this information takes time. The amount of time required to make a decision depends on how much information the brain needs, and the amount of information required depends basically on how many alternatives the brain has to choose among.

Even the simplest of perceptual decisions, like determining whether or not a light has flashed on, takes nearly two-tenths of a second. If the brain has to choose between two alternatives, say whether the light is red or green, the decision requires three-tenths of a second. Selecting among five alternatives requires five-tenths of a second, and among eight alternatives over six-tenths. It is true that some of this time is taken up in making a response—for example in saying that a light of a particular color has gone on—but this response time is the same however many alternatives are involved. What makes the difference to the delay is the number of alternatives.

But then, the amount of time required to make any kind of decision is always affected by the number of alternatives that are involved. This is another basic principle of perception with which we are all familiar. The speed with which we can recognize our own car on a parking lot depends on how many other cars are there. Even if our car is right in front of our eyes, we recognize it less rapidly if it is surrounded by other cars. In other words, the rate at which we recognize something does not depend solely on the condition of our eyes or on the nature of the object we are looking at or trying to see. Speed of recognition is affected by the number of alternatives.

Of course, we are usually not aware that we do not see everything in front of our eyes, or that a significant amount of time can elapse between looking at something and seeing it. But we are unaware because we assume we see everything instantaneously, an assumption that is itself provided by the brain. Vision, and our feelings about vision, depend far more on the brain than on the eyes.

I shall now explain how it can be shown that the brain requires time to make sense of visual information and that there is a considerable limitation upon how much can be seen at any one time. I shall also demonstrate that by making use of what we know already we can make the same amount of visual information go very much further, and therefore see very much more. The demonstrations are conveniently relevant, because they happen to involve reading.

How Not to See Very Much

I would like to put you into a situation where you can get only one glance at a line of randomly selected letters, like the twenty-five letters in the following rectangle:

JLHYLPAJMRWKHMYOEZSXPESLM

Researchers usually contrive to limit participants in experiments to a single glance by flashing the line of letters on a screen from a slide projector or computer for about one-hundredth of a second. I cannot arrange events in this book so that you will have only one glimpse of the line of letters; you are clearly free to inspect it for as long as you like. But I can ask you to use your imagination, and if you wish to check on me you can put a friend into the experimental situation by covering the rectangle with an index card. When your friend is ready, with attention focused on the center of the card, slide the card away quickly to permit a glimpse of the letters. But in the same movement bring the card back again to cover the letters once more, to prevent a second look.

The question is: How many letters can be seen in a single glance, in one brief input of visual information? Are you ready—in your imagination—while I flash the letters on the screen or remove the card for just a moment? There they were! How much did you see? And the answer is: Not very much. You saw only four or five letters, clustered around the point where you happened to be focusing. If you were looking in the middle of the rectangle, for example, you might have been able to recognize W K H M Y. You would have seen that other letters were present, but you would not have been able to say what they were.

So now we have an answer to the question of how much can be seen in a single glance, at least as far as a line of random letters is concerned. Four or five. And I must point out that this limitation has nothing to do with age, skill, or experience. One of the oldest findings in experimental psychology is that four or five letters are the *upper limit* on how much can be seen in the situation I have described. Children reasonably familiar with the alphabet perform almost as well on such a task as adults with many years' experience in reading, and practice will not make anyone very much better.

Nor does it make any difference how long the letters are flashed on the screen or exposed by the moving card, provided the observer gets only one glance. It is not the rate at which visual information gets to the eye that puts the limit on how much can be seen in a single glance, but how long the brain takes to make its decisions. Information gets to the eye, and thereby becomes available to the brain, almost instantaneously. It does not matter whether the flash on the screen (or the movement of the card) is as brief as a thousandth of a second, provided there is adequate illumination. In that instant, information from the page gets into the visual system. After that instant the brain begins to work and the eyes in essence shut down, though they may stay open. The work of the eyes is done for the moment; any additional information they might pick up will serve only to overload the brain. The fact that the visual information might be available in front of the observer's eyes for a total of a fifth of a second—fifty times as long as the minimum exposure required—will make absolutely no difference. Nothing more will be seen. The brain is too busy trying to make sense of the information that the eye collected in the first thousandth of a second or so. If you stare, it is because you do not understand what you are looking at, not because you are seeing more. Perhaps now you can understand why the exact amount of time a person is allowed to view the letters in the rectangle does not matter very much, provided it is less than the fifth of a second or more required to organize a second glance.

If four or five random letters are the most that can be seen from a single glance, it might then appear that the question of how fast we can read would depend on the speed at which we can keep glancing at a page. But you cannot speed up reading by speeding up the movements of the eyes. The limitation is not on the rate at which the eyes can pick up information, but on the rate at which the brain can "process" or make sense of that information. To examine the limited rate at which the brain can process new visual information we must probe a little deeper into the matter of how the visual system works.

Fixations

Unless they are fixed upon an object in motion that they are tracking, such as a bird or a moving finger, the eyes do not move smoothly and continuously. Instead they jump episodically from one point of focus to another. When you look around a room, for example, the eyes dart from one place to another, picking up information from a different scene every time they come to rest. The detective whose eyes sweep over a suspect from head to foot, picking up every incriminating detail, exists only in fiction. In real life the detective's gaze leaps from the suspect's nose, to the feet, to the hands, and back perhaps to the left leg before settling accusingly on the pocket in which the evidence is lodged. Incidentally, the fact that the eyes jump around when we examine a stationary scene or object helps to make the point that you see with the brain, not the eyes. No matter how fast and in what order your eyes examine the different parts of a room, in your perception the room remains coherent and stable. You do not see the constantly changing and fragmented "image" that falls on the retina of the eye, you see the room that the brain constructs. However incomplete and disjointed the information available at the eye, the brain organizes an integrated perceptual experience—if it can—that is complete and meaningful.

In reading, the eyes do not move smoothly along the lines and down the page. Once again the eyes shift around in leaps and bounds which in reading are given the technical label *saccades* (a French word meaning "jerks"). And in the jargon of reading, the periods when the eyes come to rest are called *fixations*, although the duration and function of fixations in reading are no different from those of the pauses that the eyes make in perceiving the world generally. Each fixation is a glance.

During the saccade, by the way, when the eyes are in motion, you are essentially blind, unaware of the blurred image that must sweep over the retina as the eyes move across a stationary scene. The blur is visual information that the brain ignores.

Shifting the eyes from one fixation point to another does not take very long. Depending on the angle through which the eyes have to travel, the time spent in movement ranges from a few thousandths of a second to about a tenth of a second. The average interval between fixations is about a quarter of a second so that for most of the time the eyes are stationary. As I have already explained, only the beginning part of the fixation is taken up with the eye getting information from the page and into the visual system. For most of the duration of the fixation, the brain is busy "processing." I have also said that the rate of reading cannot be speeded by accelerating the rate of changes in fixation. Both beginning and fluent readers change fixations about four times a second, which is about the rate at which children and adults glance quickly around a room or inspect a picture.

The Rate of Visual Information Processing

To recapitulate, readers change their point of fixation about four times a second, and in a single fixation can identify four or five letters out of a line of letters similar to those in the rectangle in our imaginary experiment. It might appear then that the rate at which the brain can process visual information is easily calculated: five letters per fixation multiplied by four fixations per second equals twenty letters per second. But such is not the case. The rate at which the brain can identify letters in the situation we have examined is only *four or five letters per second*. In other words, it takes the brain a full second to complete the identification of the four or five letters that can be seen in a single glance.

Researchers know that the brain requires a second to identify five letters from the visual information available from a single fixation because if they flash a second line of letters on the screen in their experiments within a second of the first, the two displays of visual information interfere with each other. If the second display of letters comes within about a tenth of a second of the first, an observer may even deny that the first display was ever presented. The longer the delay between the two displays, the more an observer is able to report seeing, but the full quota of four of five letters will not be reported from the first display unless the interval between them is a second or more. Obviously the visual information that the eyes can pick up in a thousandth of a second stays available to the brain for at least a second. But it does not look as if unprocessed visual information stays in the head any longer than a second, because there is no further improvement if the interval between the first and second displays is extended to two seconds, or three seconds, or indefinitely. Four or five random letters is the limit. To report more, the observer requires more information.

There is another kind of experimental technique that verifies the fact that individual letters cannot be identified faster than four or five a second. Six-letter words are unreadable if the letters comprising them are flashed on a screen one at a time, always in the same position so that each successive letter "masks" the one before, at a rate faster than four or five a second. In other words, at least a fifth of a second is required for the identification of successive letters when the letters can only be seen one at a time.

So now we have answers to two questions that have been raised in this chapter:

1. *There is a limit to how much can be seen at any one time, and that limit in terms of random letters is four or five.*
2. *There is a limit to the rate at which the brain can identify random letters in reading, and that rate is four or five letters per second.*

Regardless of the results that researchers claim to get in their experiments, you may object that real life vision is different. Obviously we can read faster than four or five letters a second, which would work out to a maximum reading speed of barely sixty words a minute. And indeed we *must* be able to read faster, because sixty words a minute happens to be far too slow for reading with comprehension. But I did not say that the experiments demonstrated how fast we can *read,* only that the brain can process visual information no faster than the rate of four or five random letters a second. When we read we use nonvisual as well as visual information. Now I want to show that by using nonvisual information we can make the limited amount of visual information the brain can process go much further, and thus see and comprehend much more.

The imaginary experiment must be conducted again, still with a sequence of twenty-five letters presented to the eyes for no more than a single glance, therefore making available to the brain the same amount of visual information. But this time the twenty-five letters will be presented in the form of familiar words, as in the following example:

SNEEZE   FURY   HORSES   WHEN   AGAIN

Once again you must imagine having just one glance at the letters in the rectangle, either because they are flashed on a screen for just a fraction of a second or because they are revealed to you briefly by the movement of a covering card. Are you ready? There! What did you see? And the answer this time is—twice as much as you were able to see before. When the letters are organized into words, readers can generally identify a couple of words, the equivalent of ten or a dozen letters. You would probably have seen . . . FURY HORSES . . . or . . . HORSES WHEN . . .

It is not an adequate explanation of the previous phenomenon to say that in the second demonstration words were recognized instead of individual letters. Of course they were. But you never get anything for nothing in reading, and in order to recognize the couple of words you had to process visual information that must have been contained in the letters. So we are left with the question of *how* the same amount of visual information processing that would permit you to identify only four or five unrelated letters enables you to identify twice as many letters if they are organized into words. And the answer is that you must be making the same amount of visual information go twice as far. You are making use of nonvisual information that you already have in your brain, and which in the present instance must be related to your knowledge of how letters go together to form words.

The essential point of the two demonstrations so far is that the amount of visual information required to identify a single letter is cut by half if the letter occurs in a word. The amount of visual information required to identify a letter of the alphabet is not fixed, but depends on whether the letter is in a word or not. Identification of a letter involves the brain in a decision, and the amount of information required to make the decision depends on the number of alternatives there are. So now I have to show that the number of alternatives that a letter might be varies depending on its context. I also have to show that as readers we *know* how the number of alternatives can be reduced when letters occur in words, and that indeed we can make use of this nonvisual information when we are called on to identify letters in words.

Knowledge About Letters

Suppose that instead of asking you to imagine trying to identify the original sequence of twenty-five random letters in a single glance, I had asked you to guess what each of those letters was likely to be without seeing them at all. You could justifiably object that there was no way for you to guess that one letter would occur rather than any other. That is what the word "random" means—that each letter has an equal probability of occurring, namely one in twenty-six. Any letter of that sequence could have been any letter of the alphabet. You had no basis for making an intelligent guess.

But suppose that now I had asked you to guess what a particular letter might be in that *second* sequence of letters, the letters that were arranged into English words. Or suppose that I ask you to guess what the fifth letter of the tenth line of the next even-numbered page of this book might be. Now you are in a position to make an intelligent guess—you would probably guess E, or perhaps T or A or S. It is very unlikely that you would guess Y or X or Z. And your guess would have a very sound basis, because in fact E, T, A, I, O, N, and S are by far the most frequent letters in English words, while Y, X, and Z come right at the other end of the scale. Individual letters are not all given the same amount of work to do in English words. E, for example, occurs forty times more often than Z. If you had guessed E, you would be forty times more likely to be right than if you guessed Z.

Now I am not suggesting that we read words by *blindly* guessing what particular letters might specifically be. But we can in fact use our very accurate knowledge of what letters are *likely* to be in order to exclude from consideration those letters that are unlikely to occur. This is *informed* guessing. And by excluding in advance unlikely letters, we can reduce the number of alternatives the brain has to consider so that it processes very much less information. Of course we shall be wrong on occasion, but our knowledge of how letters go together to form English words is so extensive, and so reliable, that in fact we can take the chance of being wrong occasionally in order to take advantage of the gains we make by guessing right so often.

Let me show how this process of guessing—*prediction* is a better word—can be based on sound prior knowledge. Play another guessing game with me. I am thinking of a common six-letter word. Tell me what the first letter is likely to be? Most English-speakers confronted by such a question guess one of the common letters I have already listed. In a number of informal demonstrations I have conducted with large groups of people I find that one in four or one in five guesses S—not one in twenty-six which is what the average would be if guesses were made randomly. Remember, what is important is not in fact to guess *exactly* the letter I have in mind, but *not* to guess an unlikely letter. And I get very few guesses of X or J or Z. Suppose, then, that the guess of S is correct—and indeed the six-letter word I have in mind does begin with S. What is the second letter likely to be?

Now it happens to be another fact of English spelling that letters do not follow each other at random in English words, even given their overall unequal frequencies in the language. E is the most common letter of the English language, but not after Q. Every experienced reader knows that if the first letter of a word is S, the next letter will almost certainly be a vowel or one of a limited set of consonants. The second letter of the word I have in mind happens to be T, which on the average I find one person in about three guesses correctly the first time. But I am not so much concerned with the fact that one person in three is absolutely correct as that hardly anyone makes a ridiculous guess, like J or B. People *use* their knowledge of letters and words. They guess the most probable letters, which means that their chances of being correct are high. If the first two letters are S and T, what is the third? The third letter must be a vowel or Y or R, so we are down to seven alternatives, rather than twenty-six. There are only six alternatives for the fourth letter—which happens to be E—and only two vowels and a few consonants for the fifth, which is A. STREA—can you guess what the last letter will be? Depending on the way you perceive the world (I am conducting a subtle personality test) you will guess M or K.

Have I made the point? Statistical analyses of English words show that the *average* number of alternatives that a letter could be in English words is not twenty-six, but eight. Occasionally there will be a large number of alternatives of course, but sometimes hardly any. There is no question about the letter following a Q, for example, or the missing letters in PAS— T—E SUG—R. In fact every other letter can be obliterated from many passages of English text without affecting comprehension at all. To be technical, English (like all languages) is *redundant*—there is more information available than we need. Our *uncertainty* of what a letter might be depends on the number of alternatives, and every letter contains enough visual information to identify it from among twenty-six alternatives. But because of the redundancy in our language our uncertainty about letters in English text is never one in twenty-six. What we already know about our language in advance reduces our uncertainty from one in twenty-six to an average of about one in eight.

Not only do all readers have this prior knowledge of their language—generally without being aware they have it—but also they constantly *use* the prior knowledge without being aware of it. This is why letters on distant billboards or letters that are scribbled may be impossible to identify in isolation but are quite clear in words. We have less uncertainty about what letters might be in words. Children who have been reading for less than a couple of years demonstrate the use of nonvisual information in this way. They find it easier to identify letters that are obscured in some way when those letters are in words than when the identical letters are in sequences that do not constitute words.

Where does it come from, this very specialized skill that enables us to use prior knowledge about letter probabilities in reading, even though we may be unaware of both the knowledge and its use? The answer can only lie in reading itself. The acquisition and use of nonvisual information in reading are among those essential skills of reading that I have said are never taught. Nor need such skills be explicitly taught; they are developed without conscious effort, simply through reading. After all, children have been living since birth with the universal limitation on the amount of visual information that any brain can process, and have solved the problem of identification with minimal information many times, in the process of recognizing familiar faces and objects in their world. If we are unaware of having this skill, it is because we perform it so well. Learning to acquire and use knowledge that will reduce the amount of information processing the brain must engage in is natural and inevitable.

Nonvisual Information from Sense

One more demonstration, this time to show that with one additional aspect of nonvisual information the brain can at least quadruple how much can be seen from a single input of visual information. Imagine once more the brief presentation of twenty-five letters, except that now they are arranged in a meaningful sequence of English words. Not only are the words grammatically organized, but they make sense:

EARLY   FROSTS   HARM   THE   CROPS

Are you ready? Once again one glance is all you are allowed. How much did you see? And the usual answer this time is *everything*. You did not see just part of the line, but all of it, four or five words instead of four or five letters.

There should be no need to belabor the point. The amount of visual information available to the brain in each of my three demonstrations was the same, and each time the brain had the same amount of time to process the information. If at least four times as much can be seen when the letters form a sequence of words that makes sense, it must be that the sense makes so much nonvisual information available that the visual information can be made to go four times as far. Now I must show you that readers can indeed possess prior knowledge about how words go together in English that will cut down the number of alternatives dramatically, and therefore reduce the amount of information required to identify words.

Let us play a game of guessing successive words in sentences. For example, suppose I stop writing . . .

Can you guess what the next word was going to be in the interrupted sentence you have just read? If your guess was "in" then you were correct. What might the next word be after:

Suppose I stop writing in . . .

Almost certainly you would have guessed the next word in that sequence:

Suppose I stop writing in the . . .

The next word was to have been "middle." And then "of," "a," and "sentence."

Such a demonstration takes up too much room in print. Try the experiment instead with a friend, reading a brief item in a newspaper or magazine and asking for guesses about each successive word.

I am not concerned that you or your friend should get every word absolutely right in such a demonstration. Indeed if you could predict every word exactly there would be no purpose in reading the passage in the first place. But what is necessary is that every time you are always able to make a *reasonable* guess about the next word. You do not predict recklessly. You select from a relatively small set of *possible* words in the particular context, and as a result cut down the number of alternatives among which the brain has to select. The gain is considerable.

An author can choose from at least fifty thousand, perhaps a hundred thousand, words in writing a book, in the sense that most readers can recognize on sight and understand anywhere from fifty to a hundred thousand words. And each of these words from which the author can choose obviously contains sufficient visual information that it could be identified in isolation. Put another way, each word must contain sufficient visual information to be distinguished from a hundred thousand alternatives. But in making decisions about what a particular word in the book will be, the author cannot choose from among a hundred thousand alternatives. The author cannot say, "I haven't used the word *rhinoceros* for a long time, I'll use it now." Given what the author wants to say and the language in which it is being said, the number of available alternatives is always extremely limited. The author also cannot suddenly decide to use a past participle or the passive voice. The grammatical constructions that may be employed are also limited by the sense of the message to be conveyed. In fact at any particular point in the text, an author is free to choose not among about a hundred thousand words but among an average of about two hundred and fifty.

It is knowledge of what the two hundred and fifty alternatives might be for any particular word that enables readers to read and comprehend what the author has written.

Readers have nonvisual information about the choices available to the author, and make full use of this knowledge to reduce their own uncertainty about what successive words might be. When I stopped in the middle of a sentence and invited guesses about what the next word might be, you (or your friend) would be very unlikely to have reasoned "He hasn't used *rhinoceros* for a long time so I'll try that." The guess—the prediction—would have been for a word that was *possible*. In other words, you have a reasonable idea of what an author is going to write before you read it. You are not identifying one word out of a hundred thousand every time, but one out of two or three hundred. And if you do not have that much expectation about what the next word might be, you will not be able to understand what you read, simply because you will not be reading fast enough or seeing enough at any one time. You may be reduced from seeing a meaningful four or five words in a fixation to seeing a meaningless four or five letters.

This reduction of uncertainty by the reader makes a tremendous difference to how much visual information need be processed. As much visual information as you would need to identify a single letter in isolation will permit you to identify an entire word in a meaningful context. Perhaps you cannot read the word *toast* if I scribble it by itself, but if I write "This morning I had *toast* and marmalade for breakfast" you will probably have little difficulty in deciphering it. You just do not need so much visual information when a word is in context.

In reasonably easy-to-read text, such as newspaper or magazine articles, one letter in two or one complete word in five can be eliminated without affecting intelligibility. In other words, readers know so much that for every letter the author supplies, readers can provide the next themselves, without even looking.

Tunnel Vision

By way of review let us look at the main points of this chapter in the reverse order of the demonstrations.

There is a limit to the amount of visual information the brain can handle. How much can actually be seen and comprehended in a single glance, or in an entire second of visual information processing, depends on how much nonvisual information the brain can bring to bear. If a lot of nonvisual information is available to the brain, then an entire line of type can be apprehended at once:

If only a limited amount of nonvisual information can be used, however, only half as much can be seen:

and if there is practically no nonvisual information that can be used then vision is restricted to a very small area indeed:

There is a very graphic term that is used to describe the condition illustrated in the third situation; it is *tunnel vision*. We see a line of print as if we were looking at it through a narrow paper tube.

Tunnel vision, you will notice, is not here a physical malfunction of the eyes, nor is it a consequence of any weakness in the visual system. Tunnel vision is not a permanent state; it occurs when the brain is overloaded with visual information. Tunnel vision is a condition in which beginning readers must often find themselves.

Tunnel vision is not restricted to children, however. It is not difficult to give adults tunnel vision, for example by asking them to read something that they do not understand very well. Reading nonsense causes tunnel vision, for the simple reason that nonsense is not predictable. Tunnel vision is however an occupational hazard of learning to read, partly because the beginner by definition does not have very much experience in reading. But the condition is aggravated if the print the beginner is expected to read is not very predictable, so that little nonvisual information will be available in any case.

Tunnel vision is not restricted to reading; it will occur in any situation in which the brain has to process large amounts of visual information. If you were to step on a stage and look out into an auditorium, one glance will be sufficient to tell you whether the auditorium was fairly full or not:

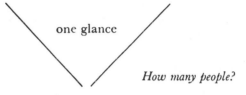

But if you were curious to see whether there were more men than women in your audience, two or three glances would be required:

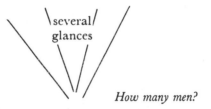

And if your curiosity led you to check whether the majority of your audience was wearing spectacles, many glances would be required:

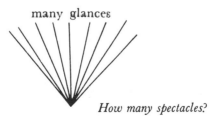

The width of your field of view does not depend on your eyes, but on how much your brain is attempting to achieve, the number of alternatives it is considering.

The information processing limitations that cause tunnel vision, by the way, affect the ears as well as the eyes. It is easier to hear what someone is saying, even in a whisper or in a room where many conversations are going on at the same time, if what is being said makes sense to you. But nonsense is much harder to hear. It is not for nothing that we raise our voices when we try to speak in an unfamiliar foreign language; difficulty in comprehension produces temporary hearing loss. Most teachers are familiar with children who seem deaf in class but can hear perfectly well outside.

Causes of Tunnel Vision

Because of the bottleneck in the visual information processing capacity of the brain, being able to read depends on using visual information economically, using as much nonvisual information as possible. But tunnel vision is unavoidable in the following circumstances:

1. *Trying to read something that is nonsense to you causes tunnel vision.* You should note that whether or not something is nonsense depends to a large extent on what the *reader* knows. If you could read Dutch, then you would have seen several words with each glance at the passage of Dutch that I gave you to read earlier in this chapter. But if the passage in Dutch was essentially random letters to you, then you would have had tunnel vision. The fact that a piece of writing makes sense to an adult, who can therefore see it easily, does not mean that the same words will make sense to a child. If something cannot be predicted, it will cause tunnel vision. Are the language and content of children's readers always predictable?
2. *Lack of relevant knowledge causes tunnel vision.* It is not necessary to throw away a book because you find it unreadable. Acquisition of a little prior knowledge from elsewhere may suddenly make the book become readable. Students who have difficulty reading science or history texts may not be suffering from a lack of reading ability. They may simply need to know a little more about science or history. Visual and nonvisual information are required for reading anything. If there is a lack of nonvisual information, then the reader must seek elsewhere to acquire it.
3. *Reluctance to use nonvisual information causes tunnel vision.* Using nonvisual information involves risk—there is always a chance you might be wrong. But if in fact you are not making occasional errors when you read, you are probably not reading

efficiently. You are processing more visual information than you need. Errors need not be a cause for concern in reading, provided the reader is using appropriate nonvisual information. Such a person reads for meaning. And if we read for meaning and make a mistake then the sense of the passage usually tells us when the mistake we have made makes a difference. (If a mistake makes no difference, then what difference can it make?) Thus a good reader is quite likely to make quite conspicuous misreadings sometimes, like reading "apartment" rather than "house." And such a reader will not self-correct unless the misreading makes a difference to meaning. This is the way fluent readers read. A poor reader on the other hand might pay far more attention to visual aspects of the task and mistakenly read "horse" for "house." Such a reader will not be likely to self-correct, although this time the error makes a considerable difference to sense, because the meaning is not being attended to in the first place. A common characteristic of poor readers in high school is that they read as if they do not expect what they read to make sense, as if getting every individual word right was the key to reading. But the more they try to get every word right, the less they will see, the less they will understand, and the worse their reading will be on every count.

The greatest cause of reluctance to use nonvisual information sufficiently is *anxiety*. Hence my advice at the beginning of this book to relax as you read it. In any situation in life, the more anxious we are about a decision, the more information we require before that decision is made. And in reading, you just cannot stop to collect large amounts of visual information in order to make your decisions. Anxiety causes tunnel vision, and tunnel vision eliminates any likelihood of comprehension.

4. *Poor reading habits cause tunnel vision.* If you read too slowly you will get tunnel vision since the visual system will become clogged with all the visual information you are trying to get from the page. If you are reluctant to push ahead, if you read and reread in a hapless endeavor to remember every detail, then you will get tunnel vision. If you strive to get every word right before you look at the next, you will get tunnel vision. Unfortunately, these bad reading habits are sometimes deliberately taught in the belief that they will help children to read. The problem for many children who experience difficulty becoming readers is not that they cannot be taught, but that they learn too readily. They have been too much influenced by a teacher who misguidedly says, "Slow down, be careful, and make sure you get every word right."

Overcoming Tunnel Vision

Cures become obvious once causes are apparent. Might children have tunnel vision because what they are expected to read is nonsense to them? Then the teacher should ensure that what the children are expected to read makes sense to them. (And a "readability formula" will not work this out for teachers; the problem is too relative. What is lucid to one child may be completely unpredictable to another. But there is a simple solution. If children would not understand something even if it were read to them, there is no way they will make sense of it when trying to read it for themselves.)

Might children have tunnel vision because they have insufficient prior knowledge of what they are required to read? Then they must be given the necessary prior knowledge in some other way—from other books that they *can* read, or by a lecture, a film, or even by having some or all of the book they are expected to read read for them first of all. Reading ability will not be improved by reading tasks that are impossible.

Might children have tunnel vision because they are afraid of making a mistake? Neither comprehension nor learning can take place in an atmosphere of anxiety. Prediction, like learning, is a risky business and a child must feel that the risks are worth taking. Children who are afraid to make a mistake will not learn, and will not even demonstrate the reading ability that they might have acquired. Reassurance must be the basis of "remedial" instruction for readers experiencing difficulties at any age.

Might a reader have tunnel vision because of poor reading habits? The secret of all speed reading courses is fundamentally this—to force the reader to read fast. Slow reading is a bad habit, but many people read slowly because they are afraid they will not comprehend if they speed up. Speed reading courses aim to show that fast reading is efficient reading. Their students are forced into situations where tunnel vision is impossible; the reassurance they get as their vision and comprehension open up provides the basis for more efficient reading generally.

Summary

We do not see everything that is in front of our eyes, and we see nothing immediately. It takes time for the brain to decide what the eyes are looking at. Reading depends more on what is behind the eyes—on *nonvisual information* than on the *visual information* in front of them.

Excessive reliance on visual information can overwhelm the brain's decision-making ability and result in *tunnel vision,* when only a few letters rather than entire phrases can be seen at one time. Tunnel vision is most likely to occur when what is read makes little sense to the reader or when the reader is anxious about making mistakes. Neither closer attention to the text nor increasing the fixation rate will make reading more efficient or make learning to read easier.

3

Problems and Possibilities of Memory

There is another reason why reading must depend on the eyes as little as possible. If we are too concerned with the print on the page in front of us, we will probably forget what we are reading as we read it. I am not talking now about being unable to recall what we have read an hour or a day or a week later, though this is an aspect of memory I shall discuss later in this chapter. I am talking about forgetting what we read almost immediately, so that we cannot even understand it, let alone recall it subsequently. I am talking about forgetting the beginning of a sentence before we get to the end of it, so that it can make no sense. Or even—if we are unfortunate enough to be afflicted with tunnel vision— forgetting the beginning of a word before we get to the end, so that we cannot even decide what a particular word is.

Forgetting where you are in the middle of a word is not an uncommon phenomenon. We all experience it occasionally when we try to read or pronounce unfamiliar long words, especially in a foreign language. The same difficulty arises when we cannot get past the middle of a complex mathematical formula, or fail to remember completely a new address or telephone number when we have nowhere immediately convenient to write it down. In each of these cases the kind of memory that seems to be overwhelmed is not the memory that we call on when we want to recollect something that happened days or months ago. Rather it is a more temporary memory that is required so that we can make sense of what we are doing at the moment. This kind of "working memory" may be called *short-term* memory, to distinguish it from our *long-term* memory of events long past. Both kinds of memory are important in reading. Both have limitations as well as strengths. I shall talk first about short-term memory and then about long-term memory.

Limitations of Short-Term Memory

Short-term memory can be very easily overloaded, or over-whelmed, and a sure way to do this in reading is to try to fill short-term memory with too much detailed information from the page.

Information about the world around us flows into and out of short-term memory all the time we are conscious, even though we are normally not aware of the process at all. But if someone you were listening to suddenly stopped and asked, "What were the last half-dozen words I said?" you could always give the answer, provided you had been paying attention. Suddenly cover the page or close the book while you are reading and you will find that you can always recapitulate the last few words you have read. Ask someone who is watching a sporting event or a film for a description of the most recent action, and it can usually be provided. Always there seems to be a residue of the immediate past in the forefront of our minds that we can recover if we are asked, although we are rarely aware of having it. This "instant playback" of the immediate past is short-term memory; it is not very different from what is often called *attention*. Short-term memory is, in fact, everything we happen to be paying attention to right now, including our own intentions.

Incidentally, these examples all show that in one sense memorization is never a problem at all. Everything to which we are paying attention seems to get into the head briefly. The difficulty is not memorization but forgetting—the information that gets into the mind does not stay or we cannot find it when we want it.

Forgetting is not usually a problem with short-term memory, however, because we rarely want the information it contains to stay for very long; only while we make sense of what we are doing or complete what we are trying to accomplish. We may want to remember the words at the beginning of a sentence until we get to the end of it, but no longer. Imagine the clutter in your head if you remembered every word you saw or heard, no matter how trivial or irrelevant it might be. Short-term memory clears itself automatically to allow us to proceed with the next item of business.

Short-term memory, in other words, is our working memory, which contains what we happen to be attending to. It then clears so that we can continue with the next task. It is rather like an internal scratchpad where we jot down a few notes relevant to a current problem and then erase so that we can work on the next one.

Human short-term memory is such an efficient system that we are rarely aware of its limitations, and therefore rarely aware that it exists.

Short-term memory does have shortcomings, however. There is a limit to how much it can hold and a limit to how long its contents can be retained.

Suppose you have just looked up a new number in the telephone directory and try to dial the number without a second look in the book. You usually find that you can just about hold the seven-digit sequence in your mind provided that you do not have to give any attention to anything else. If someone asks if you have the correct time, the telephone number has gone. If the operator asks for your own number you lose track of the one you are trying to call. Short-term memory, in other words, has a capacity for about six or seven items. It is as if a benevolent providence equipped us with sufficient working memory to hold a telephone number, but failed to predict area codes.

Short-term memory also has a very limited duration. We can remember the six or seven items only as long as we give all our attention to them. The technical term for the deliberate way in which we try to keep something in short-term memory is *rehearsal*. We can retain the unfamiliar telephone number for just as long as we are able to rehearse it. The moment we turn even part of our attention elsewhere, something is lost.

For as long as we pay attention to what is in short-term memory, on the other hand, we cannot attend to anything else. Once again we will be essentially blind, even with our eyes open, if we pay so much attention to detail that we have no room for new information in short-term memory. The contents of short-term memory, in other words, represent our complete experiential world at any particular time. If we want to make sense of what we are attending to at that particular time, we must be able to make sense of the contents of short-term memory.

Perhaps you can now see why tunnel vision in reading is such a disaster from a short-term memory point of view. Earlier you might have thought that the problem of tunnel vision could be easily over-come—that if you can see only four or five letters at a glance rather than four or five words, then all you need do is read slower. But anyone who can identify only four or five letters in a fixation is going to find out that four or five letters just about fully occupies short-term memory at any one time. (Given that part of short-term memory must always be occupied with the general control of the task we are involved in, it might be said that the information acquired from a single fixation in reading will completely fill short-term memory.) There is no way that any reader will be able to comprehend if attention is restricted to four or five letters at a time, perhaps forgetting E . . . L . . . E . . . P . . . while working on . . . H . . . A . . . N . . . T, or losing track of the first half of a sentence before getting into the second half. Comprehension gets lost in the bottleneck of short-term memory the moment we worry about getting individual words right, or become afraid that we might miss a significant detail.

Overcoming the Limitations of Short-Term Memory

It may sound as if I am arguing that reading is impossible, if roughly half a dozen items is the most we can hold in short-term memory at any one time, and attention to four or five or even six letters is not enough to enable us to make sense of print. How is the bottleneck overcome? The answer must be that reading is not a matter of identifying individual letters, or even individual words. When we are reading with comprehension, we must not be bothering short-term memory with letters or even words at all. We avoid overloading short-term memory by paying minimal attention to all the incidental detail of print.

Go back to my earlier observations about the limited capacity of short-term memory. I said it could hold no more than six or seven *items* but I did not say what those items had to be. Short-term memory will just about hold the seven *digits* of an unfamiliar telephone number, or it will hold the same number of unrelated *letters*. But it will also hold half a dozen *words*. And if we can put half a dozen words into short-term memory then we can in effect retain twenty-five or thirty letters. We can make short-term memory look much more efficient if we can organize small detail into larger units. This organization is sometimes referred to as *chunking*. The capacity of short-term memory is not so much six or seven items as six or seven *chunks*. A word is a chunk of letters. I can give you a chunk of a dozen digits that you could easily hold in short-term memory and still have capacity left over for more— *123456123456* or *888888888888*. Will the letters *CHEVAL* fill short-term memory for you? It depends on whether you understand French. If you know that *CHEVAL* means "horse" you will have room in short-term memory for *CHEVAL* and five or six other items. But if *CHEVAL* is meaningless to you then short-term memory will be filled.

Now you have another reason why comprehension is so important in reading and in learning to read. A chunk is a meaningful organization of elements—it is in fact something you know already. The reason the word *HORSE* is so much easier to hold in short-term memory than the same number of unrelated letters, or that *1234567* is easier than *7425163*, is that you are familiar with sequences already. It is not so much that the letters or digits are ordered that makes them easier to attend to as the fact that you are familiar with the order; you have it in your head already so you do not have to put it all in short-term memory. The familiar organization is another aspect of nonvisual information. You overcome the limitations of short-term memory in reading by making the most sense you can out of what you are looking at. You do not worry about letters if you can make sense of words. Worrying about letters will make word identification difficult; trying to read nonsense will make reading impossible.

Short-Term Memory and Meaning

I have said that the capacity of short-term memory is six or seven items, six or seven letters, or six or seven words. But we can hold units larger than words in short-term memory; we can fill it with rich chunks of *meaning*. Now it is difficult to say exactly how big a meaning is because meanings are not amenable to being separated and counted or measured in the way letters and words are. And it takes a little time to explain what meanings are because it is in the nature of meanings that they go far beyond mere words, a complication that will be the topic of my next chapter. But it is not difficult to demonstrate that we can hold meanings in short-term memory instead of individual words, and that the equivalent of many more than six or seven words can be held in short-term memory if they are organized meaningfully.

For example, the limitation to six or seven on the number of words that can be held at one time in short-term memory only applies when the words are truly independent unrelated items; a "list" of words such as *imagine with who begun the forget contents*. But if the words form a meaningful sentence at least a dozen can often be recalled without error. And sentences of twenty words or more can usually be repeated immediately after a single hearing, not perfectly but at least with no omissions or changes that affect the basic meaning—compelling evidence that it is meaning rather than the particular words that we hold in short-term memory.

The only way to read is at the level of meaning, and the only way to learn to read is at the same level. Unfortunately students are often expected to read material that is not meaningful to them (no matter how much sense it makes to the teacher). Moreover, children are often expected to *learn* to read with material that is not meaningful to them. Some producers of instructional materials even make a virtue out of the fact that their products are nonsense, since it inhibits children from committing the supposed offense of "guessing." But all that nonsense does and can do is cause tunnel vision and a log jam in short-term memory.

Material that is meaningful—that can be related to what a child or student knows already—is essential if reading skill is to be developed. But meaningfulness may not be enough. One of the tragedies of some reading instruction is that children are sometimes encouraged to read sense as if it were nonsense. They are told to make sure to get all the individual words right, and to slow down and figure out the hard words letter by letter when they run into difficulty. The problem with this type of instruction is that all too often it is successful. Children can learn that reading is not a matter of making sense but of getting every word right. Older students characterized as having severe reading problems typically behave as if they have no expectation that what they are trying to read will make sense. They have learned too well the destructive lesson that reading with comprehension should take second place to word accuracy. Being able to recognize words on sight is a skill that comes with reading, not a prerequisite. Like any kind of sight recognition—birds, stars, cars, airplanes, trees—it comes with experience.

Limitations of Long-Term Memory

Short-term memory is not sufficient for all our needs; it may be uniquely adapted for holding a telephone number that we intend to call in the next minute or so, but we can hardly rehearse a number continuously if we do not plan to dial it for a week. Short-term memory is the location for information that we intend to erase, but what about information that we want to keep? The knowledge and beliefs that are part of our more or less permanent understanding of the world are contained within the aspect of memory that is called *long-term*. Long-term memory is the source of the all-important non-visual information in reading that I have been talking about. In the next few pages I want to explain my statement at the beginning of this book that the effort to memorize—to put new information into long-term memory—may completely destroy comprehension.

Long-term memory is quite different in many respects from short-term memory. At first glance it even seems to compensate for all the shortcomings of short-term memory. For example, short-term memory has very limited capacity—six or seven items—but the capacity of long-term memory appears to be literally inexhaustible. No one need ever fear that it will be a waste of time trying to learn something because long-term memory is fully occupied already. There is no need to erase from your mind the name of an old friend to make room for the name of a new one. Long-term memory seems always able to expand to accommodate new information that we want to put into it.

Moreover, the contents of long-term memory seem to persist indefinitely. While the contents of short-term memory slip away the moment our attention is distracted, nothing in long-term memory seems ever to be forgotten. Sometimes events that we have not thought about for years are suddenly brought to mind, perhaps by an old photograph or a snatch of song, or perhaps by a particular taste or smell. All our senses seem capable of revivifying old memories for us, memories we might have thought we had lost forever.

You might object that long-term memory may be boundless and permanent in theory, but in practice it is often difficult to recall things that you tried to memorize even quite recently. But there is a distinction between *memorization,* or getting something into long-term memory, and *retrieval,* getting it out again. And here we confront the first great limitation of long-term memory, the fact that its contents are rarely immediately accessible.

Unlike information in short-term memory, which is at once available for recall, information in long-term memory requires rather more positive action to get it out. It can be most frustrating when we have almost recovered something we want from long-term memory but still it manages to elude us. What was the name of that restaurant that served such delicious desserts? You know it was a two-syllable word, and it probably began with a K, but the rest is tantalizingly out of reach. Was it the Kingsway? No, but how can you tell what a memory is *not* if you cannot tell what it is? Obviously the memory is there locked away in some manner, but you haven't found a key that fits. One of the keys would be the sought-for word itself. The moment somebody gives you the correct name, or you suggest it to yourself by running through possibilities, you are able to say "Aha, that is it."

The critical difference between short-term and long-term memory can be summed up in one important word—*organization.* Short-term memory holds unrelated items, but long-term memory is a network, a structure of knowledge, it is coherent. Long-term memory is everything we know about the world, and everything we know about the world is organized. We not only know that there are twenty-six letters in the alphabet, we know their names, their order, and how they go together to form words. Our friend George is a teacher, like several other people we can name, and he has a dog that we know must have four legs and a tail. We can assume that George, being a teacher, knows there are twenty-six letters in the alphabet, but that his dog does not. Everything we know is related to everything else. Try to think of two things that cannot be related in terms of a third. Nothing in our knowledge of the world can be completely unrelated to anything else that we know, in fact it could not be "knowledge" if it were.

When we add to our knowledge of the world, when we learn, we either modify or elaborate the organization of information that we already have in long-term memory. Organization, in other words, is synonymous with "making sense." Anything we try to learn that cannot be related to the structure of knowledge we already have in long-term memory is meaningless to us. It is nonsense. And there are several good reasons why no one should ever be in the position of having to try to learn or memorize something that is nonsense. One good reason is this: *it is only through organization that information can become established in long-term memory, and it is only through organization that it can be retrieved again.*

Organization is the key to recall, as every student who struggles to memorize "facts" ought to know. To recall anything you have to get to it through the network. You must probe among the kinds of things it might be related to. To get the name of the restaurant, try in your imagination to walk along the street that it was on, see if you can "see" the sign. The better we have something organized in long-term memory, the easier it is to retrieve. That is why recent events, especially those that happen to be particularly relevant to us, are usually easier to recall; they are more closely related to so many of our immediate concerns. The reason most of the memories of our childhood seem to have gone, except for the rare occasion when some particular stimulus quite unpredictably jogs our recollection, is that we view the world now with a different frame of reference. We have lost contact with our younger days. To recall what the world was like as a child, it must be seen through the eyes of a child.

This matter of the organization of knowledge in long-term memory is one that will occupy us again, at greater length, when we consider the nature of meaning and comprehension. But for the moment we should not be diverted any longer from our examination of the differences between short-term and long-term memory, for we have come to the most critical one of all: the rate at which new information can be put into long-term memory is very slow indeed.

Short-term memory, you will recall, has a limited and transient capacity, but at least information goes in and can be brought out practically instantaneously. You should start rehearsing the moment you find out the telephone number that you want to ring because the number is in short-term memory as soon as you have read it or heard it. But entry into long-term memory is extremely laborious and time-consuming—*it takes four or five seconds for one item to become established in long-term memory.* To put a telephone number into long-term memory, so that you can call it after lunch or in a week's time, requires a good half-a-minute of concentration, four or five seconds for every digit.

Now you can see why long-term memory cannot be employed to make up for the limited capacity of short-term memory. To transfer even a single letter or word into long-term memory requires five seconds of concentration, an ultimate bottleneck that seals the fate of any attempt to read that involves an overemphasis on visual information.

This final bottleneck explains why the effort to memorize can completely destroy comprehension in reading. Every time you try to cram another detail into long-term memory, so that you may be able to answer some of those awkward questions afterwards, you distract your attention from the text for at least five seconds. In such circumstances comprehension is impossible, and if you are trying to read without comprehension, what use is memorization in any case?

Overcoming the Limitations of Long-Term Memory

I have been as imprecise in talking about long-term memory as I was with short-term; I have been saying that you can put only one "item" into long-term memory every five seconds. But just as an item for short-term memory may be a letter, a word, or even a meaning, so an item for long-term memory can be a chunk as large as we can meaningfully make it.

Obviously reading will be disrupted if we try constantly to feed into long-term memory isolated and unrelated bits of information like single letters or individual words. But meanings (the meaning of a sentence or the meaning of a paragraph) can go into long-term memory as well, and it takes no longer to put a rich and relevant chunk of meaning into long-term memory than it does a useless letter or word.

The way to overcome the bottleneck of long-term memory, therefore, is the same as the solution to the problem of limited capacity in short-term memory and to the problem of tunnel vision in processing visual information. The material that you are reading must make sense to you in as meaningful a way as possible.

I must now make two brief points that are relevant at this time but which will be discussed in more detail later. The first is that we should not require to put a lot of new information into long-term memory when we read. There is a difference between comprehending something that we read and committing it to memory. We make use of information that we already have in long-term memory in order to comprehend, but because of the bottleneck we do not bother to put into long-term memory a second time anything we already know. That is one reason we usually have a relatively poor recollection of books that are easily comprehensible, the relaxing paperbacks that do not make us think very much. They are easily comprehensible because they are largely predictable. We know a good deal about them in advance, and therefore we do not commit very much to memory. I am not saying we should not remember major points of what we read, although I believe memorization is rarely as important as many teachers insist. But it must be recognized that memorization exacts its price in reading. To expect a good deal of memorization, especially of material that is not easily comprehensible in the first place, is to make a very high demand on a reader indeed.

My second point, I am happy to say, is considerably more positive. Having stressed how the effort to memorize will interfere with comprehension, I can now present the other side of the coin—*comprehension takes care of memorization*. The best justification for the preceding statement is to describe an actual experiment.

Three groups of people are put into exactly the same experimental situation. Each individual is given a pack of fifty index cards to study for a fixed period of time, say twenty minutes. On each card is a common word, a "concept" like *horse, tree, butterfly, justice,* or *running.* People in the first group are told simply to sort the cards into separate piles on any organizational basis they like. There are no restrictions, provided they make at least two piles and fewer than fifty. In other words, members of this group are expected to think about the words on the cards. Asking them to sort the words in some manner is a cunning way of asking them to relate words on the basis of what they already know, to make the words "meaningful." The actual manner in which the cards are organized is in fact irrelevant to the study, and is not examined, because the researchers are really concerned with memory. An hour after the conclusion of the twenty-minute sorting task, when the participants think the experiment is over, the real purpose is suddenly thrust upon them. They are asked to recall as many of the fifty words as they can.

Unfair, you may say. If the purpose of the study is memorization, why not tell the participants what to expect? This is precisely what is done with the second group. They are given exactly the same cards and the same sorting task, but they are also warned in advance that a memorization test will follow. *But this additional instruction makes no difference.* The group that is required to organize as well as to memorize does no better on the memory task than the group that is simply asked to organize. In other words, the organization—the comprehension—takes care of the memorization.

Perhaps you will now object that the second group is asked to do too much, to organize as well as memorize. A third group in these experiments is not given the "irrelevant" task at all, but is simply told to examine the cards for twenty minutes because an hour later they will be given the memory task. They have the worst recollection of all. Simply trying to memorize results in the least memorization.

Memorization and Anxiety

Thus far I have emphasized meaningfulness. I have asserted that the memory bottlenecks can be overcome in the same way as the visual bottleneck, by reading material that makes sense. But there are also questions of attitude.

A piece of reading material may be capable of making eminent sense to prospective readers, yet still prove impossible for them to read. One reason, as in the case of tunnel vision, may be anxiety. Readers who are afraid of making a mistake as they read, of not comprehending every detail, will overload short-term memory and confuse themselves into complete bewilderment. And readers who try to cram too much into long-term memory will not only find that they have nothing to remember for their efforts, but also succeed in transmuting sense into nonsense in the process.

Why should any reader be so anxious about memorization that any possibility of comprehension, let alone enjoyment, is destroyed? One has only to consider the emphasis on tests and memorization in many school situations to find an answer. Indeed, the common procedure known in schools as a "comprehension test" is usually an imposition on long-term memory, since it is given when the reading is over. The emphasis on memorization precludes the very thing the test is supposed to measure. High school students desperately anxious about their own reading ability may be given a free choice of books by well-meaning instructors and sent off with the blessing "Just relax and enjoy it—I'll only ask you one or two general questions when you've finished." Imagine now the students trying to second guess the instructor, trying to retain a mass of unimportant detail in the vain hope of covering the "one or two general questions" that might be asked. The innocuous request: "Just tell me what the book is about" may prove no less monstrous; summarize *War and Peace* in a couple of well-chosen sentences.

Unreasonable demands by others when we learn to read may lead to inappropriate reading habits later. Many adults seem to read—even when they are alone and "reading for pleasure"—as if they expect a sadistic examiner to trap them on every trivial point when they are finished. If they have trouble comprehending a sentence they go back and reread it ten times, rather than going forward to ignore or even resolve the uncertainty.

No one who is afraid of the consequences of reading will be able to read, and no one who is afraid of failing to read will learn to read. A sure way to give children a reading problem is to tell them that they have one.

But there is more to reading than vision and memory, necessary and important though they both are. There is more to reading even than a tranquil state of mind. We have still only looked at reading from inside the head, through the reader's eyes, so to speak. It is time to change the perspective and look at a completely different aspect of reading—its function as *language*.

Summary

Long-term memory is our relatively permanent knowledge of the world. Short-term memory is a transient store for what we happen to be attending to at any particular time. Both aspects of memory have critical limitations that can disrupt reading and learning to read. Only a few things can be held in short-term memory at any one time, handicapping any reader who relies on visual information. Entry of new information into long-term memory is slow, and interferes with comprehension. Both limitations are easily overcome if the reading material is meaningful, provided also that the reader is not unduly anxious about making mistakes or about failing to remember detail. For learners especially it is crucial that reading materials make sense.

4

Shallows and Depths
of Language

Limitations of memory and bottlenecks in the visual system are two reasons why readers should not rely too exclusively on the print in front of their eyes. There is a third reason: it is not in print that the meaning of written language lies. I recognize that this opening remark might sound paradoxical. Surely the whole point of reading is to get meaning from the written or printed words? But my aim in this chapter is to show that readers must bring meaning *to* print rather than expect to receive meaning *from* it. I want to show that there is a difference between the "visual information" of the print we see on the page and meaning.

Reading is widely perceived to be simply a matter of "decoding to sound," of translating the basic elements of written language, the letters, into their equivalent sounds in spoken language. Meaning is then assumed to be instantly available in these sounds of speech that the reader imagines hearing, just as the meaning would be apparent if the reader were actually listening to someone else reading aloud. But there are two critical objections to these assumptions. One objection is that my opening point about meaning having to be brought to written language rather than from it applies to spoken language as well. A listener must supply meaning just as much as a reader must; meaning is not unambiguously provided in either a written or spoken utterance. It follows from this assertion that even if readers were able to decode written language into speech, they would still be confronted by the problem of trying to determine meaning for what had now become spoken language.

The second objection—which I shall deal with first—is that in any case it is not possible to decode written language into speech, at least not without comprehending the written language in the first place. And if it is necessary to comprehend written language before decoding it into speech, then of course it is not necessary to decode into speech at all. We can read—in the sense of understanding print—without producing or imagining sounds.

The argument that writing cannot be translated into speech without prior understanding undermines one of the most hallowed and widespread educational dogmas—that the way to teach reading is to teach *phonics*. I want to show that phonics, which means teaching a set of *spelling-to-sound correspondence rules* that permit the "decoding" of written language into speech, just does not work. To expect any readers, and especially beginners, to learn and rely upon phonics is to distract them with involved and unreliable procedures that are in fact largely unnecessary. Not only does the development of fluency in reading demand very little in the way of prior knowledge of spelling-to-sound correspondences, but the practice of reading itself provides the implicit understanding of those correspondences that readers require.

If we examine first the nature of the relationship between letters and sounds, we shall be in a better position to see that rather than phonics making reading possible, it is reading that makes phonics seem to work. In the process of criticizing phonics as an instructional method, I shall try to indicate how many children seem able to learn to read despite the phonics instruction they receive.

THE FALLACY OF PHONICS

The issue concerns the number and nature of the correspondence between the letters of written language and the sounds of speech. There would be a perfect "one-to-one correspondence" between the two aspects of language if every letter stood for just one sound and every sound was represented by just one letter. Then indeed we might help children to read by getting them to learn the rules of spelling-to-sound correspondence. In the same mechanical way we could also employ computers to convert written language into speech, to the great advantage of the blind. All that is needed is a program of spelling-to-sound correspondence rules to connect individual letters that can be "recognized" by the optical systems already available for computers to devices for synthesizing the sounds of speech, with which current technology can also equip computers. The reason phonics does not work for children or for computers is that the links between the letters and sounds cannot be uniquely specified. Both must have entire words—or large parts of them—in their memory before they can recognize words, which makes individual spelling-to-sound correspondences largely redundant. The problem is not that the correspondences are not known, but that they are too complex. They are not one-to-one.

For a start, our written language is provided with an alphabet of just twenty-six letters while there are about forty distinctive sounds in our spoken language. Obviously some letters must correspond to more than one sound. In fact, there is not one letter in our alphabet that is not associated with more than one sound (or with silence, like the *k* in *knot*). Nor is there any single sound of speech that is represented by only one letter. Spelling-to-sound correspondences are not one-to-one, but many-to-many. And there lies the core of the problem of phonics for human readers and for computers—to know which of the many-to-many correspondences should apply on a particular occasion. There may be half a dozen alternative ways of pronouncing individual letters, and no reliable phonic guide as to when each of the alternatives applies.

Some simplification can be achieved by recognizing that we cheat with our alphabet and use it as if there were in fact more than twenty-six letters. This expansion is achieved by employing combinations of letters to represent sounds that are certainly not combinations of sounds corresponding to the letters considered independently. For example, the various sounds we give to the letter combination *th*—like the sounds at the beginning of *thin* and *this*—are in no way blends of any possible sounds of *t* and *h* considered separately. Some alphabets are a little more straightforward about such matters. Greek, for example, has the single character "theta" (θ), for the initial sound in *thin* which English represents by a two-letter combination. In the same way, the Greek alphabet has the single character "phi" (ϕ) for the sound we represent by the two letters *ph* at the beginning of *phone*. But then English also has the single letter *f* for the same purpose.

Because of the tendency of English to use combinations of letters for sounds that cannot be considered combinations of single letter sounds, linguists prefer not to regard the twenty-six letters of the alphabet alone as the basic elements of written language. They talk instead of a larger set of *spelling units* that includes all twenty-six single letters and a number of combinations of letters as well. Many combinations of vowels are regarded as spelling units because, like such consonant combinations as *ph*, *th*, and *sh*, they behave differently when they are together than they do when they are by themselves. The vowel sound in the middle of the word *coat*, for example, cannot be regarded as a combination of the vowel sounds in the words *cot* and *cat*, any more than the vowel sound in the middle of *cook* can be regarded as two occurrences of the sound in the middle of *cot*.

At first glance, the idea of regarding certain combinations of letters as basic units of written language, with spelling-to-sound correspondences of their own, might appear to be nothing but advantageous. Certainly, the more letters that are taken into account at one time, the fewer correspondences there are likely to be. The letter *o*, when considered by itself, can be involved in about a dozen different pronunciations, but for the spelling unit *oo* there are only three correspondences (as in *brook, broom,* and *blood*) while the combinations *ook* and *oom* (but not *ood*) have only one. *Th* has two pronunciations but *thr* only one. However, the argument that spelling-to-sound correspondences become simpler as the sequences of letters considered as units become longer demands some restraint, otherwise one finishes up asserting that readers need to consider whole words as a unit before trying to pronounce them, which demolishes the rationale for using phonics in the first place. And even at the level of entire words there is not always a one-to-one correspondence. Some words like *read, lead, wind,* and *wound* have different pronunciations for the same spelling, while other words have different spellings for the same pronunciation, like *so, sow,* and *sew,* or *their* and *there.* Moreover, another insoluble problem for human readers and for computers expected to decode on the basis of phonics alone is having to decide whether certain combinations of letters should be regarded as spelling units or not. There are no phonic rules to indicate whether *th* should be regarded as a single unit as in *father,* or as two separate letters as in *fathead.* How can the different functions of *ph* be distinguished in *elephant, haphazard,* or *shepherd,* or *sh* in *bishop* and *mishap*?

Because decisions about what constitutes a spelling unit of English are quite arbitrary, estimates of the number of spelling units that written English contains vary widely among different theorists, from fewer than fifty to over seventy. One might think that with about fifty spelling units in written language and forty sounds of speech, a one-to-one correspondence between the basic units of writing and speech might come closer. But such is not the case.

An exact figure cannot be given for the number of correspondences that have been identified between spellings and sounds in English because the number of correspondences goes up with the number of words examined. An analysis of 20,000 quite common English words revealed a total of over 300 correspondences.

This total cannot be reduced very much by cutting down on the number of words, especially as it is the common words of our language that contribute most of the complexity—such words as *the, of, was, their, money, horse,* and *enough.* Over 200 correspondences were discovered in an analysis restricted to only 6,000 of the commonest words, namely all the words of one or two syllables occurring in a survey of the spoken language of children aged between six and nine. (Another 3,000 words in the survey were ignored because they were three syllables or more in length and too complicated for the analysis, though obviously not too complicated for the children to understand.) Nevertheless, in the 6,000 items that were the shortest and simplest words in the everyday language of these children, the researchers still found no fewer than 211 different correspondences. Eighty-three of these correspondences involve consonants, which are generally thought to be relatively straightforward, 79 involve just the six vowels when they occur alone—*a, e, i, o, u,* or *y*—and the remaining 49 correspondences involve combinations of vowels.

There we have a measure of the complexity of the spelling-to-sound correspondences of our language, the system that phonics aims to teach in the form of "rules" for decoding writing to sound. Not only is the system massive and complex, it is also unreliable, because it contains no way of predicting when a particular correspondence applies. What is the use of a complex set of rules if there is no reliable guide for when a particular rule should be employed?

It may be argued that many of the 211 correspondences should not be regarded as rules but rather as "exceptions." But such a distinction plays with words. One could argue that only twenty of the 211 correspondences should be considered rules, and that the other 191 correspondences were exceptions. But then the burden of remembering the exceptions would be greater than the economy of remembering the rules. Alternatively it could be argued that only ten or a dozen of the correspondences were exceptions—but then there will be about 200 rules. The researchers who analyzed the 211 correspondences in the 6,000 children's words made the quite arbitrary decision that 166 of these correspondences should be regarded as rules and 45 as exceptions—and then found that their decision made exceptions of more than 600 of the most common words in the language.

Furthermore, there is no rule that will tell a child whether a word should be regarded as an exception or not, and what is the point of remembering a lot of rules if you have to recognize a word before you can tell whether it follows the rules or not?

It does not help to say that phonics may not be perfect but it gives a reasonable idea of how a word is likely to sound. A rather generous estimate gives correspondence rules, on the average, a chance of being right three times out of four. But the chance is with one *sound*. The average word has at least four sounds in it, and a one-in-four possibility of error on single sounds goes up to three-in-four over sequences of four sounds. The appropriate pronunciation will be produced only 25 percent of the time. This is the fallacy underlying phonics—the belief that there actually could be a set of rules that work efficiently to decode written language into sound. The computers that appear able to do this do so largely by recognizing whole words.

I am not trying to exaggerate. The spelling-to-sound correspondences of English are so confusing that in my judgment children who believe they can read unfamiliar words just by "blending" or "sounding" them out are likely to develop into disabled readers, the type of secondary students who are condemned for being "functionally illiterate" because they do exactly what they have been taught and try to read by putting together the sounds of letters.

Besides, I think it would be difficult to exaggerate the complexity and unreliability of phonics. To take just one very simple example, how are the letters *ho* pronounced? Not in a trick situation, as in the middle of a word like *shop,* but when *ho* are the first two letters of a word? Here are eleven common words in each of which the initial *ho* has a different pronunciation—*hot, hope, hook, hoot, house, hoist, horse, horizon, honey, hour, honest.* Can anyone really believe that a child could learn to identify these words by sounding out the letters?

Incidentally, the preceding illustration underlines an important requirement of phonics that is never explicitly taught at school—that phonics requires reading from right-to-left. The eleven different pronunciations of *ho* that I have just given all depend on the letters that come next. The pronunciation of *g* or *p* or *k* at the beginning of a word depends on whether the second letter is *n.* The right-to-left principle has very few exceptions—*ash* and *wash, mood* and *blood, host* and *ghost*—and is observed though rarely acknowledged in one of the first phonics rules taught at school: that vowels in the middle of a word "say their name" if the word ends with "silent e," or however else the difference is taught between *hat* and *hate, mop* and *mope.*

Making Phonics Work

How then can one account for the tremendous popularity of phonics? I think one explanation is that many people simply think that phonics *should* work; after all, words are made up of letters, and what are the letters for if readers are going to ignore them? I shall reply to that argument in a moment. But first I want to show that phonics gets credit for efficiency that it does not deserve. I want to show that there is in fact a rule that can ensure that phonics will work. The rule is very simple: phonics works if you know what a word is likely to be in the first place.

I am not being facetious. Once you recognize a word as "hotel," you do not need to wonder about the other ten pronunciations of *ho* that are possible; in fact, it will probably not occur to you to think of them. You are not likely to consider all the different ways a word *might* be pronounced if you already know how it *is* pronounced. Therefore phonics always looks obvious to people who can read. It is not surprising that children who are best at phonics are the best readers— they have to be. A cynic has said that the smartest children keep one phonics lesson ahead of the teacher—and the smartest teacher keeps one phonics lesson behind the children.

The fact that you need to know what a word might be in order to make sense of phonics is employed in some of the more sophisticated attempts to develop rules for transforming written language to sound. Some linguists, for example, recognize that spelling-to-sound correspondence rules are easier to apply if the meaning of words is taken into account. They point out that the different role of the *th* in *father* and *th* in *fathead* is easy to detect if it is taken into account that *father* is one word and *fathead* two. Put another way, phonics works if you understand the word in the first place. The researchers working on the 211 correspondences described above devised a simple rule for distinguishing the "short a" at the beginning of words like *about, adore,* and *ago* from the "long a" at the beginning of words like *able, acorn,* and *apron.* Since all these are words of two syllables, the first consisting of just the single letter *a,* it might be thought that there is no way of distinguishing among them. But there is a rule; it depends on how the word is stressed. If the emphasis is on the first syllable, as in *able,* the *a* is long; if the word is stressed on the second syllable, as in *about,* the *a* is short. So the researchers in all seriousness included "intonation rules" in their phonics program. In plain English, if you want to know how a word is pronounced, say it.

Phonics will in fact prove of use—provided you have a rough idea of what a word is in the first place. If you know that the word you are looking at is probably *horse, cow,* or *donkey,* phonics will enable you to tell the difference. But here you do not have to run through all eleven alternatives for the first two letters of *horse*—you just have to know that a word beginning with *ho* could not be "cow" or "donkey." And you certainly do not have to work your way through the entire word, "blending" all the possible combinations of sounds.

Of course, to be able to make some reasonable prediction about what a word might be, you need to be able to make sense of what you are reading. Here is another reason why learning to read is so difficult if it involves something that makes no sense to you. How can you tell what a word might be if you have no understanding of what you are reading?

Reading Without Phonics

A last-ditch defense of phonics in the face of the analysis I have just presented runs sometimes like this: how is it that people are in fact able to read if the spelling-to-sound correspondences of our language are really so cumbersome and unpredictable? This kind of circular argument begins with the assumption that reading needs phonics and takes the fact that reading is possible as proof that phonics must work. To counter such an argument it must be shown not only that phonics is ineffective but also that phonics is unnecessary. It must be shown that readers can recognize words and comprehend text without decoding to sound at all.

How is it possible to recognize written words without sounding them out? The answer is that we recognize words in the same way that we recognize all the other familiar objects in our visual world—trees and animals, cars and houses, cutlery, crockery, furniture and faces— that is, "on sight." We can recognize the thousands of words with which we are familiar for the same reason that we can recognize all the thousands of other things, because we have learned what they look like. (The actual process by which the visual recognition of words and objects takes place will be discussed in more detail in the next chapter, when again we shall discover that there is no need to postulate any processes that are exclusive to reading. Nor is there any fundamental difference between the way we *learn* to recognize objects and the way we learn to recognize written words.)

The fact that written words are made up of letters that seem in themselves to be related to sound is as irrelevant to their recognition as the fact that most automobiles have their model name stuck on them somewhere. Most people can distinguish a Jeep from a Volkswagon without having to look for the manufacturer's label. We recognize the written word *car* in the same way that we recognize a picture of a car or even a real car, by what we have learned about how the entire configuration looks. And just as we can recognize familiar cars and other objects from a glimpse of just part of the object, we can often recognize written words from a glimpse of just part of them. As I explained earlier, ease of recognition depends on how much you know in advance.

It might be thought that written words look pretty much alike, and that it would be harder to distinguish words like *car* and *house* than it would be to distinguish an actual car or house. But this is not the case. Researchers who measured how long it took experimental viewers to say "house" when the written word was suddenly presented in front of their eyes found that the reaction was faster than when they were shown a picture of a house. Viewers even respond faster in reading the word red, yellow, or blue written on a sheet of paper than in saying the same word when the entire sheet of paper is colored in the appropriate color.

Furthermore, it is not necessary to say what a word is to comprehend its meaning. Quite the reverse; it is often necessary to comprehend the meaning of a word before you can say what it is. In other words, *meaning* is directly related to the spelling of words rather than sound. How otherwise could we be aware of many spelling mistakes? The reason a teacher corrects *their* to *there* in the phrase *Go over their, please* is not because the spelling *their* represents the wrong sound—it obviously does not—but the wrong meaning. *Pair, pare,* and *pear* all "decode" to the same sound but each spelling has a different meaning that we recognize on sight. It is easier to understand the sentence *Eye sea too feat inn hour rheum* if it is read to you than if you read it yourself; the sounds may be appropriate but the spellings indicate quite different meanings. But then, recognizing the meaning of something, recognizing *what it is*, always comes before giving a name to it. We do not have to say "There's an airplane" before we can comprehend that the object is a plane. Rather, we have to recognize what the object is before we can give it a name.

Millions of people succeed in reading languages that do not have an alphabet, where there is no possibility of reading a word unless it is recognized on sight. Languages like Chinese, for example, are *ideographic*—the written words are symbols for ideas, but not for specific sounds or even specific words. Thus speakers of the different Mandarin and Cantonese Chinese spoken languages, who cannot understand each other's speech, can still write to each other. They both understand that a particular written symbol means "house" even though they have different spoken words for it. In the same way English and French speakers can understand 2 + 2 = 4 even though one might not understand "Deux et deux font quatre," and the other might not understand the English alternative. In English it is usually regarded as an error to read the word *small* as "little," but such a "mistake" would be impossible in Chinese, where it would be no different from interpreting the sign + as "add" rather than "plus." After all, we have no difficulty in attaching meaning directly to the spoken words that we know. Why should there be a unique difficulty in attaching meaning to written words? Fundamentally there is no difference; meaning and print are related in the same manner as meaning and speech, and neither language form is dependent upon the other.

It may be objected that expecting a reader to recognize and comprehend written language directly, without first decoding to speech, would overburden memory. Isn't it unreasonable to expect children to learn to recognize and distinguish thousands of different words on sight, instead of simply memorizing a set of rules for transforming written language into speech that is already understood?

But there is no evidence that there is any limit to the capacity of human memory. The "overloading" argument mistakes the very nature of memory, regarding it as a kind of store in which items are piled up on each other, rather than as a network, a system that can only function better with a richer interconnection of parts. If anything, adding new and meaningful elements to memory increases its efficiency. The main limitation of the brain lies in its restricted capacity to handle new information, to attend to current events. Having to deal with too much at any one time causes tunnel vision and overloads short-term memory. The brain prefers to depend on decisions that it has made in the past rather than having to perform complex tasks repeatedly.

Children memorize all the time, so effortlessly that we are not aware that they are doing it. Only nonsense is difficult to memorize. In the first ten years of their lives children develop a spoken language vocabulary that enables them to recognize and make sense of at least 20,000 words, which means an average learning rate of 2,000 words a year, nearly eight words a day. At the same time children are also acquiring the knowledge that enables them to identify on sight hundreds of faces and many thousands of objects; to recall ages, birthdays, telephone numbers, addresses, and prices; to sing songs and master the rules of games; to find their way around buildings, streets, and fields. The number of different objects we learn to distinguish and recognize is uncountable. Among such a multitude, the memorization of written words, with all the meaning that can be brought to them, is a rippling stream that loses significance as it becomes part of a broad river.

The Function of Spelling

Why then have letters? If letters do not efficiently code to sound and can trap the unwary reader into the functional blindness of tunnel vision, why have the dangerous things around at all? I think there is a simple explanation. Letters are a convenience for producing written language.

Writing is much more demanding than reading, even in a narrow physical sense. Readers can flick their eyes over pages of type for hours on end without bodily fatigue, but writers must plod their way through every word, pushing their pencil or pen forward at barely a tenth of the speed that readers achieve. Even writers who employ electric typewriters and word processors are constrained to putting their thoughts on paper at a much slower rate than the brain can comfortably produce them. Writers who use dictaphones lose the main advantage that writers have over speakers, immediate and easy access to what they have already said. Besides, the alphabet was invented before the tape recorder and it serves to assist the secretary and printer as well as the creative writer.

The biggest memory problem for writers is in fact shared by typists and printers as well, namely the need to put words into visible form so that readers will be able to recognize them. A distinction must be drawn here between two different facets of memory retrieval—*recognition* and *recall*. To recognize an object you merely have to observe that it is in some way familiar. In effect, the very object that you are looking at serves to jog your memory; often the merest glance will suffice. But recall demands reproduction of the whole thing; much more effort and information is required. (Think how easy it is to recognize that a spoken word or name we have been trying to think of is the right one, compared with the strain of trying to bring it to mind in the first place.) A fluent reader will attend to only a fifth or less of the "visual information" that is on the page, but the writer has had to put it all there. The reader can skip but the writer must remember and put in every detail. *Reading* printed words in Chinese is no more difficult than reading them in English, although the Chinese symbols do not decode directly to sound; the process of immediate recognition is the same. But *writing* is much harder in Chinese than in English because of the many thousands of different characters. Learning to *recognize* thousands of different forms is not such a big achievement, but learning to *reproduce* them is.

As a result, alphabets have been developed to help writers and printers remember how words should be reproduced. Thousands of complex forms have been reduced to a couple of dozen simple elements. And these elements themselves, the letters of the alphabet, are to varying degrees predictable from spoken language. Even if writers do not remember how to spell occasional words correctly, they can usually make an approximation that will tell a reader what was meant.

The mere fact that the alphabet can be employed to reduce the complex visual configurations of words into more simple elements is a help to teachers as well as to writers; it facilitates talking about how written words should look. Instead of saying, "There's a kind of goalpost at the beginning then a big circle and a vertical stroke with a bar over the top" you say, "Spell it H-O-T." The simplification of thousands of complex words into a few letters made printing possible in the days when all type had to be moved by hand or accommodated within the visual span of a keyboard. The demands of the typewriter industry played a large part in the development of a phonetic alphabet for Japanese, after the failure of other attempts to fractionate words so that their parts would fit on a manageable number of keys. Similar endeavors are helping to make reading materials more available in China, but they will not necessarily make the act of reading any easier for the Chinese.

Readers do not need the alphabet. For centuries people have learned to read without knowing a thing about letters, and millions still do. Our Western phonetic alphabet was developed when written language moved out of the exclusive domain of the church and university, where the emphasis was on reading and interpretation, and into commerce where every merchant wanted to write explicit records and send out unambiguous bills. It is perhaps not coincidental that the invention of our alphabet has been attributed to the Phoenicians, the traders of the ancient Mediterranean world.

However, writers have not been permitted to get away with a completely phonetic alphabet. The spelling of words is never a direct and unvarying representation of their sounds, and for several good reasons. First, written language is not permitted to vary with dialect (in fact it represents no one's *actual* spoken language). We do not normally expect writers to reproduce words in exactly the way they hear them spoken in their part of the world or speak them themselves. A person may speak quite distinctively as a Texan or a New Englander, a Scot or a Cockney, but we do not expect these idiosyncrasies to show up in the spelling of words, no matter how they charm the ear. The spelling of words is a *convention* that crosses hundreds of dialect boundaries; attempts to reproduce dialect in written form do not make reading easier, even when the dialect reproduced is supposed to be our own. Liberty to spell the name of Shakespeare in seventeen different ways may have taken a slight memory load off Elizabethan writers, but the preference of readers for consistency has prevailed since. In fact, written language is much more consistent than speech over time and distance. Reading the plays of Shakespeare today would be much more difficult if they were written to reflect the sounds of the English that Shakespeare spoke.

Another reason why spelling is not a direct reflection of the sounds of words is more fundamental. It is not basically the function of spelling to represent sound, but to represent meaning. Take some everyday examples. To make a singular written word into the plural we simply add an *s*—*dog–dogs, cat–cats, judge–judges.* (I am ignoring the "irregular" plurals like *child–children, man–men, sheep–sheep.*) But the written *s* we add is an indication of meaning, of plurality, not of sound, because in speech we pluralize *dog* by adding the sound /z/ ("dogz"), *cat* by the sound /s/ ("cats"), and *judge* by adding /iz/ ("jujjiz"). Would reading be simplified if we had three general plural endings, *s, z,* and *iz,* that more exactly reflected sound, instead of just one? There are many other examples. The past tense of *walk* is pronounced "walkt," the past tense of *hug* is pronounced "hugd," and the past tense of *mend* is pronounced "mendid," but the single past tense meaning that is represented by three different sounds in speech— /t/, /d/, and /id/—is represented by the single suffix *ed* in writing.

This tendency of spelling to remain consistent for a particular aspect of meaning despite considerable variation in sound can be summed up in a single principle—*words that look alike tend to mean alike.* It is this principle that makes sense of the *g* in *sign* and *assign*— the *g* is not present because of any phonic rule about how the words "sign" and "assign" are pronounced, but because *sign* and *signature, assign* and *assignation* are related words—they share a common element of meaning. The silent *g* does not reflect an aberration of the written language but a peculiarity of speech; it is a help to the reader because of what it says about the meaning of these particular words. It might be said that the spelling of these words makes more sense than their pronunciation. In the same way there is no need to appeal to elaborate phonic correspondences to account for the fact that the letter *c* sometimes has a /k/ sound, as in *medical,* and sometimes an /s/ sound, as in *medicine.* The letter *c* occurs in the middle of both words because it is part of the root *medic* representing a meaning that the two words have in common. The *c* in the middle of *critical* and *criticize* is similarly part of a shared meaning though not a shared sound. The word *nation* is part of the word *national* despite a marked pronunciation change. Of course, if you try to teach children that the letters in words are supposed to stand for specific sounds then they will see no sense in the spelling of any of the examples in this paragraph. But if the relationship between appearance and meaning is explained then the spelling of words becomes a help rather than a hindrance, not just in the recognition of words but in their comprehension as well.

In the face of the above arguments, the effort of many well-intentioned people to "reform" the spelling of English may be seen to lose some of its point. Would it really help readers to change spelling to *medisin* and *medikal?* Would it make reading (and writing) easier to write *they hugd, kist, and congratulatid each other?* Instead of *buoy,* should some people write *boy* and others *booie,* depending on the dialect they speak? Should some people spell *caught* as *cot* but others as *court?* Does it make more sense to leave the *b* at the end of *bomb* or to change the spelling to *bom* and then have to explain where the *b* suddenly comes from in the middle of *bombard* and *bombardier?*

There is a corollary to the principle that words that look alike tend to mean alike; it is that words with *different meanings tend to look different.* There is no question about the differences in meaning between *their* and *there,* or among the hundreds of other pairs of words that share the same sound in speech but have different meanings that are indicated by different spellings, such as *pair, pare,* and *pear; bear* and *bare; mail* and *male; pail* and *pale; meet, mete,* and *meat;* and *so, sew,* and *sow.* Would there be any advantage in introducing additional ambiguity into written language by spelling words with different meanings in the same way?

Of course it might be argued that a revised spelling need not be made completely dependent on sound; no system of spelling or writing reform tries to provide an *exact* written representation of all the sounds of speech, otherwise every different speaker would spell words in a different way. But if in effect you would have to learn a new dialect of spoken language, simply to understand the sounds that a modified written language is supposed to decode to, then the advantage of revising written language in the first place becomes obscure. The opinion of linguists who have made an intensive study of the relationships among spelling, speech, and meaning is quite unequivocal: the present spelling of English offers the best system for the unambiguous representation of meaning for all the various dialects of spoken English that exist.

It is a mistake to think that the "rationalization" of spelling would help even in the teaching of reading. Such a change would be regarded as useful only by those people who maintain that the main purpose of reading is to decode letters to sounds and that comprehension is a secondary consideration.

Meeting New Words

A final defense of phonics is often this: even if it is true that someone who knows how to read has no need to decode to sound in order to recognize familiar words, what about words that are not familiar? What happens when readers, especially beginners, encounter a word that has never been met before; surely then there is no alternative to phonics?

But ask competent readers how they react when they meet a word they do not recognize on sight. Usually three alternative courses of action are specified, with a very definite order of preference. The first alternative and preference is to skip over the puzzling word. The second alternative is to guess what the unknown word might be. And the final and least preferred alternative is to sound the word out. Phonics, in other words, comes last, and with good reason, for phonics is the least efficient choice.

If you now look at children—or ask them—to discover what they do when they encounter unfamiliar words, even children who are struggling through their first attempts to make sense of written language, you are likely to find a similar pattern. Children who are on their way to becoming readers behave in the same manner as fluent readers. Their tendency is first to skip, second to guess, third to sound out. If phonics is the first or only choice it is because children are reflecting what they have been taught, not what helps them to read.

Skipping is by no means as inefficient or even undesirable as it might sound as a strategy for reading. Texts that are comprehensible in the first place—that are not nonsense—remain comprehensible even if up to one word in five is completely obliterated. The identification of every word is not necessary for comprehension to take place. On the contrary, stopping to try and figure out every unfamiliar word the moment it is encountered serves only to produce tunnel vision and overload short-term memory. Comprehension is bound to be lost in such circumstances and learning becomes impossible. The tendency to stop dead at the first difficult word and thus to struggle uncomprehendingly through print a word at a time is a characteristic of poor readers of all ages. Even if it transpires that an unfamiliar word must be identified in order for comprehension to proceed, it is generally better to read past the difficult word and then go back. The two best clues to any word, if no help is available from any other source, are its total *context*—the meaning in which it is embedded—and its similarity to words that are already known.

Normally a word that is skipped is not ignored altogether. As subsequent reading clarifies the sense of the passage as a whole, so a grasp of the sense of the whole contributes toward comprehension of words that have been left unidentified. As we shall see, this use of context to throw light on new words is the way in which most new words are learned by all readers.

Guessing has a bad reputation in education and especially among reading teachers, partly through misplaced puritanism—it may suggest that children need not apply themselves properly to their "work"—and partly because guessing is regarded as synonymous with a reckless lack of thought. But guessing, as I am using the term, is not a matter of blind impetuous behavior, but rather the fundamental process of *prediction* to which I have already referred, employing prior knowledge (nonvisual information) to eliminate unlikely alternatives. Guessing in the way I have described it is not just a preferred strategy for beginners and fluent readers alike; it is the most efficient manner in which to read and learn to read.

Prediction—the elimination of unlikely alternatives—makes the third alternative for word identification possible. A knowledge of phonics will never enable children to deduce the identity of a word like *horse* (eleven alternative pronunciations of *ho* . . .) unless they can use context to narrow the range of possibilities. The best way to work out the sound of a new word is not by trying blindly to use phonic rules but by analogy with known words of a similar spelling (or more precisely, similar appearance). Indeed, the similarity of a new word to words that are already known provides clues to both meaning and sound; it is the words that are known that makes phonics seem effective with new words.

There is, however, yet another method of finding out the identity and meaning of unfamiliar words. It is the simplest method of all, and children will make as much use of it as they are permitted. This is the method of asking somebody what a word is. Children know that the important part of learning is not finding out what a word is in the first place—the *identification* problem—but learning how to recognize the same word on future occasions. Children can take care of the *recognition* problem if they are not handicapped in identifying what a word is in the first place. Identification is not usually a difficulty, at least not before a child gets to school. Until that time an obliging adult is generally on hand who will tell a child what a word is *when the child wants to know:* "this word is 'Shell,' that word says 'Stop,' and that one says your name." All these words are *meaningful,* you will notice, at the time they are learned. The parent does not write "Stop" on a chalkboard, stripped of all purpose and relevance. The word *stop* means "Stop" when it is part of a traffic sign; it is a word with utility, not just an empty sound.

But at school, suddenly, the situation is likely to be reversed. The teacher may say, in effect, "Good news and bad news today, children. The bad news is that no one is ever going to tell you what a written word is again. You will have to find out for yourselves. The good news is that you are going to learn phonics, one hundred and sixty-six rules that cannot be relied on for common words. . . ." Identifying words for children does not make them lazy, it enables them to devote more attention to the central problem of word recognition. As soon as children can use context to give them clues to new words, they quickly wean themselves from their dependence on adults, a dependence that they find time-consuming and progressively less necessary. It is through *sense* that children learn to read, and until they read well enough to make sense of what they are doing, someone must help them. Children learn to read by reading, but not all at once. They take over gradually, while other people help them at the difficult early stages. I am not suggesting that children need to learn long lists of words or to be taught words in isolation in order to read. The learning of words themselves comes easiest with meaningful reading.

It is difficult to exaggerate how much any fluent reader has learned by reading. Most people who can read have a "sight vocabulary" of at least 50,000 words; they can recognize 50,000 words on sight, in the same way that they can recognize cars and trees and familiar faces, without any sounding out. How did they learn those 50,000 words? Fifty thousand flashcards? Were there 50,000 occasions when they stopped to figure out a word letter by letter, sound by sound? Or even 50,000 occasions when they asked a helpful adult to identify a word? Words are learned by reading, just as speech is learned through an active involvement in spoken language. No formal *exercises* are required, simply the opportunity to make sense of language in meaningful circumstances.

Not only do children learn to recognize words by reading, they acquire a practical working knowledge of phonics at the same time. Phonics does not make sense if a child must learn that the letter *c* sometimes has an "s" sound and sometimes a "k" sound, that it may be absorbed into a third sound in "ch" or remain silent after *s*. But once children can see the letter *c* in action in words, like *medicine, medical, church,* and *science,* they can make sense of the observation that *c* may have various relationships to sound. Now they can see these relationships for themselves and they will start discovering further relationships as they look for similarities among written words.

Children look for relationships among *words,* not just between letters and sounds, and with good reason. As we have seen, similarities in the appearance of words give the best clues to their meaning, and thus for their identification. And in the process of predicting the identity of unfamiliar words, clues based on similarities to known words combine with clues from context to permit every reader to go even further and learn the meaning of words never encountered before, in writing or in speech.

Think of all the thousands of words every adult knows. We are not *told* the meaning of every one of these words, and it is unlikely that we have made 50,000 trips to the dictionary. We have acquired the larger part of our vocabularies by hearing words spoken in meaningful situations or reading words written in meaningful contexts. Most people know perfectly well the meaning of a number of words that they cannot pronounce—a certain indication that they acquired this meaning while reading, by a process of prediction and confirmation. If we are reading for sense we can afford to take chances in predicting the meaning of words, for the thread of what we are reading will surely prove us right or wrong. Children do more than learn about reading when they read, they learn about language. All this will be further explored in the following chapters.

THE PROFUNDITY OF MEANING

Obviously, meaning would seem to lie at the core of any analysis of reading. Yet I said at the beginning of this chapter that it is not in print—nor even in speech—that the meaning of language lies. If there is to be any comprehension, it must come from the meaning that a listener or reader *brings* to the language being attended to. To explain the paradox and also its resolution it is necessary to plunge a little deeper into the nature of language itself.

Two Aspects of Language

There are two ways in which we can talk about language, whether spoken or written, and these two ways have nothing to do with each other at all. On the one hand, we can talk about the *physical character-istics* of language—about the loudness or duration or number of pauses in a passage of speech, or about the size of type or number of letters in a piece of written text. On the other hand, we can talk about *meaning*.

When we want to talk about the physical characteristics of language, references to meaning are not merely unnecessary, they are irrelevant. If you assert that someone has just been talking loudly for five minutes, I cannot object that either the loudness or length of the speech would depend on whether the topic was bananas or battleships. A sentence printed in italic type is printed in italic type, whether or not it is perceived as true or false. To make statements about the physical characteristics of language, it is not necessary to specify or even know the particular language concerned. Statements about meaning, on the other hand, can be made quite independently of any statements about physical characteristics. A critical remark is a critical remark, whether it is spoken or written. A lie does not become truth by being shouted rather than whispered, or by being printed in one type rather than another.

It is a little awkward to have to use the phrase "the physical characteristics of spoken and written language" whenever the topic is language in general, so linguists have coined a useful expression in its place; they talk of *surface structure*. The surface structure of speech might be regarded as the sound waves that pass through the air, or along telephone lines, from your vocal apparatus to my ears; it can be easily quantified by clocks and other measuring devices. The surface structure of written language can also be measured in a variety of ways; it is the ink marks on the page or the chalk marks on the board. The surface structure of written language is the "visual information" that our eyes pick up in their fixations in reading.

Surface structure is contrasted with *deep structure*, which is an alternative term for meaning. The metaphorical difference between deep and surface structure is particularly appropriate since meaning— deep structure—indeed lies at a level far below the superficial aspects of language. There is far more to language and its comprehension than is immediately apparent to the eye or ear at the shallower levels of print or sound. In fact—and this is the first of the main points I want to make in this section—there is a good deal in the deep structure of language that is not in the surface structure at all. Surface structure and deep structure are not mirror images of each other. They are not opposite sides of the same coin. Instead there is a gulf between them. There is no "one-to-one" correspondence between the surface structure of language and deep structure. The physical aspects of language, the print or the sound, contain insufficient information to convey meaning unambiguously.

The Gulf Between Surface Structure and Meaning

Here is a simple demonstration of the absence of a direct correspondence between surface structure and deep structure: one surface structure may have more than one deep structure, and one deep structure may have more than one surface structure. Put another way, differences in meaning can exist with no difference in the physical characteristics of language, and the physical characteristics of language may vary without any difference in meaning.

An example of a surface structure with more than one deep structure is: *Visiting teachers may be boring.* Who is visiting, the teachers or the person being bored? The same printed words have two meanings. Intonation will do nothing to make unambiguous the previous sentence, or any of the following: *The chicken was too hot to eat; sailing boats can be a pleasure; she runs through the sand and waves; the shooting of the hunters was terrible; father is roasting in the kitchen; mother was seated by the bishop; Cleopatra was rarely prone to argue.*

In the preceding examples, every sentence could be interpreted in more than one way; no surface structure corresponded uniquely to a single deep structure. The argument does not depend on the fact that I might have seemed to have specially picked a few unusual and not particularly entertaining puns. Ambiguity is a constant and unavoidable facet of all our language (and it will be revealing to consider, as we shall do later in the chapter, why readers or listeners are so rarely aware that this ambiguity exists).

To show that a single deep structure, a single meaning, can be represented by more than one surface structure requires no strain at all. Any paraphrases will make the point: *The dog chased the cat* and *the cat was chased by the dog* are quite different surface structures, but they represent the same meaning, and so does *le chien a chassé le chat* and innumerable other sentences that could be composed in English and any other language. The fact that any statement can be translated, and even paraphrased in the same language, illustrates the point made in the previous chapter on memory, that meaning lies beyond mere words. It makes sense to say that *he is unmarried* and *he is a bachelor* have the same meaning, but not to ask for another sentence that somehow crystallizes what the meaning of both statements is.

Comprehending Sentences

How then are sentences to be understood? If meaning is not inherent in surface structure, and surface structure is all that passes between writers and readers (or between speakers and listeners), where does the meaning come from? The only possible answer is that readers or listeners must provide meaning themselves. To justify such an answer it will help to examine in a little more detail why conventional explanations of language comprehension cannot work.

The most common explanation of how sentences are understood is probably that we put together the meanings of the individual words. But comprehension cannot be as simple as that, otherwise there would be no difference between a Maltese cross and a cross Maltese, or between a Venetian blind and a blind Venetian, The saying "Time flies" could be taken as a reference to a type of pest that infests clocks and watches, as fruit flies do fruit, or an instruction to an official at an insect race. Likewise, hot dogs could be overheated canines. Evidently we are doing more when we understand a sentence than putting together the meanings of each word. And the difference cannot be simply a matter of the order in which the words occur. The first word of *Man the boats* and the first word of *Man is gregarious* are the same, but they have quite different meanings. Rather than the words giving meaning to sentences, it looks as if the sentences are giving meaning to the words.

It cannot be argued that order plus *grammar* accounts for the meaning, because grammar itself often cannot be determined until some meaning is allocated to the sentence. To know the grammatical function of the first words in *Man the boats* and *Man is gregarious*, the entire sentences must be understood. "Flies" is a verb in *time flies* and a noun in *fruit flies*. Is *Mother was seated by the bishop* a passive sentence (meaning the bishop showed mother to her seat) or is it an active sentence (meaning she was sitting beside him)? Only when you know what the sentence is supposed to mean can you say what the grammar is.

The underlying problem in all the previous examples is that words themselves have too many meanings. Just think of some of the common words of our language: *table* (dining or multiplication?), *chair* (a seat or an office?), *office* (place or position?), *club* (weapon or organization?), *sock* (clothing or blow?). These words were not specially selected for their multiple meanings. The difficulty is to think of words that do *not* have more than one sense. Once a word gets into common use, it tends to be given as many meanings as possible; this is a characteristic of all the world's languages and seems to reflect the way the human brain works best, using a few elements very productively rather than using many elements in a restricted manner. To confirm the point, just check in the dictionary for common words like *come, go, take, run, walk, house, hand,* and see how many different meanings they have, often running to several columns, compared with the two- or three-line definitions required by less familiar words. You cannot even tell the grammatical functions of many common words when you take them in isolation—*sock, run, walk, house, fence, bottle*. All can be verbs as well as nouns. Many other words can be nouns and adjectives (*automatic, green, cold*), or verbs and adjectives (*narrow, double, idle, empty*). Some words can have three grammatical functions (*paper, light, sound*).

The most common words in English are prepositions, and these are used with the greatest number of senses. One dictionary lists 63 different senses for the word *of,* 40 for *in,* and 39 each for *at* and *by.* These words are just about untranslatable from one language to another, unless you understand at least the phrase in which they occur. The meaning of the word *by* is obvious each of the five times it occurs in the sentence *I found the book by Dickens by chance by the tree and shall return it by mail by Friday*—but could you say what the word *by* means?

Bridging the Gulf

To summarize, neither individual words, their order, nor even grammar itself, can be appealed to as the source of meaning in language and thus of comprehension in reading. Nor is it possible to decode from the meaningless surface structure of writing into the sounds of speech in order to find a back route into meaning. Instead some comprehension of the whole is required before one can say how individual words should sound, or deduce their meaning in particular utterances, and even assert their grammatical function. I am not saying that any utterance can be taken to mean anything; with most utterances only one interpretation is intended and usually there is little argument about the interpretation that should be made. But this agreement does not explain how decisions about meaning are reached and how the essential ambiguity of surface structure is overcome.

Clearly, ambiguity poses no problem at all for the *producer* of language, for the speaker or writer. Presumably speakers and writers have a reasonable idea of what they are saying in the first place, and provided they produce some surface structure that is not incompatible with their intentions, they never suspect that their words might have some alternative interpretation. For producers of language, the intended meaning always comes first, in a general sense at least, and it is difficult for them to contemplate other meanings. This is why speakers and writers are so often surprised when their audience does not find their remarks transparently clear. Speakers and writers are the last people to be aware of the puns they may unintentionally produce, or of the distortions of their meanings that are possible, and tend to be embarrassed and even annoyed when these "misinterpretations" of what they say are pointed out to them. Meaning is self-evident when we are speaking and writing, and it is difficult to accept that it does not reside limpidly in our very words, but is rather lodged securely and perhaps even impenetrably in our heads.

How then does the recipient of language manage to attribute meaning to speech or written text? Why is it that readers and listeners are usually no more aware of possible ambiguity than the writer or speaker who produces the language they comprehend? There can be only one answer—in reading or listening we approach language from the same perspective that we employ when we write or speak; the meaning must come first. If the discussion is about logarithms or transportation schedules, we never consider that *table* might refer to a piece of furniture. If the topic is horticultural blight, we do not even contemplate that *fruit flies* might be a noun and a verb. *Harold is cooking in the kitchen* must mean that Harold is doing the cooking; *chicken is cooking in the kitchen* must mean that the chicken is being cooked. Listeners often have as much trouble seeing puns as speakers, and may respond to them with a similar outrage. Everywhere we look for sense, and in language we have a good idea in advance of what the nature of that sense is likely to be. In the expectation of a particular sense, we have little difficulty in discarding or being completely unaware of potential nonsense. We may not be able to predict exactly what a writer or speaker is going to say, but we know enough not to consider unlikely alternatives. If we know so little of what others are talking about that we can make no predictions of what they are likely to say, it will not be possible for us to comprehend them in any case.

Meaning always has priority. Begin to read a book or magazine article to a friend, then stop suddenly and ask for a repetition of what you have just said. You will probably find that your listener's short-term memory is not filled with the exact words you have just read, although you will be given back a similar meaning to what you have said in more or less the same words. It is easy to show that children pay more attention to meaning than to actual words as well. Try to correct a child who says "I ain't got no candy" by asking him to repeat "I haven't got any candy" and he is likely to repeat "I ain't got no candy" until one of you quits through exasperation. If you appeal, "Can't you even hear what I'm saying?" the answer probably would have to be no—in a literal sense. The child does not hear the surface structure of your words but rather perceives a meaning that is returned to you in the child's own words. Children find the literal imitation difficult when the language they are expected to copy is not their own. Since their primary concern is with meaning, it may take them a long time to realize that someone might want them to engage in the nonsensical task of repeating *sounds*. There is no sense in surface structure. Similarly a child who reads "John didn't have no candy" when the text is "John had no candy" may well be reading more efficiently than a child who is more literally correct.

Stated baldly, the assertion that the comprehension of language is not the converse of its production—that readers do not derive meaning from print by an opposite process to that of the writer who put the meaning there originally—may sound too facile. From where do we get this special skill that enables us to comprehend language by bringing sense to what we are about to hear or read in the immediate future? The next chapter will examine how the generation and testing of predictions is the way we comprehend everything in life. Language does not require a special skill in order to be comprehended. Rather, it draws upon a general ability that any individual exhibits from the first weeks of life. Prediction is not a new and artificial skill that has to be learned but the *natural* way to make sense of the world.

Summary

Two further reasons why nonvisual information is of prime importance in reading and in learning to read have been discussed. First, reading is not a matter of decoding written symbols to sound. The system of "phonics" is both cumbersome and unreliable, and only rarely produces an accurate pronunciation for a word not recognized on sight. Better ways of identifying unfamiliar words exist, such as asking someone, using clues from context, and making comparisons with known words of similar construction. Context clues, which all children use extensively in their spoken language experience, can only be employed in reading if the material makes sense. Reliance on phonics—on "spelling-to-sound" correspondence—is dysfunctional in fluent reading and interferes with learning to read.

The second reason for the critical importance of nonvisual information in reading is that meaning is not directly represented in the *surface structure* of language, in the sounds of speech or in the visible marks of writing. Readers must bring meaning—*deep structure*—to what they read, employing their prior knowledge of the topic and of the language of the text. Once again, this use of nonvisual information is not possible if the material being read does not make sense to the reader.

5

Comprehension—The Basis of Learning

Comprehension depends upon prediction. To justify such an assertion requires more than a sentence or two. Comprehension cannot be explained in a few words. Instead we must again take a general look at the way in which the brain functions. To understand reading one must understand the brain.

So far the brain has been considered mainly in terms of its limitations as it labors to make sense of incoming information from the world around, for example the constant risk of tunnel vision when the brain tries to handle too much visual information, and the limited capacity of short-term memory. I have also tried to show that the way in which we perceive the world is largely determined by what we know and expect, just as we overcome the brain's limited capacity to handle new information by making maximum use of everything we know already. Now I must talk more explicitly about what it is that "we know already," and how we use it. I shall examine what it is—from a psychological point of view—that we carry around all the time in our head. What we already have in our head is our only basis for both making sense of the world and learning more about it.

What is it that we have in our heads, that we carry around with us all the time in order to make sense of the world? It is not sufficient to answer "memories," because the human brain is not like a souvenir album filled with an assortment of snapshots and records of past events. At the very least we would have to say that the brain contains memories-with-a-meaning; our memories are related to everything else that we know. But it is also not sufficient to say that our heads are filled with knowledge, in the sense of an accumulation of facts and figures; the brain is not like an encyclopedia or catalog or even like a library, where useful information is filed away under appropriate headings for ready reference. Certainly the human brain is not a vault in which the products of instruction are deposited when and if we attend to our teachers and our textbooks. Instead, what we have in the human brain is a *system,* an intricately organized and internally consistent model of the world, built up as a result of experience, not instruction, and integrated into a coherent whole as a result of continual effortless learning and thought. We know far more than we were ever taught.

What we have in our heads is a *theory,* a theory of what the world is like, and this theory is the basis of all our perception and understanding of the world; it is the root of all learning, the source of all hopes and fears, motives and expectations, reasoning and creativity. This theory is all we have; there is nothing else. If we can make sense of the world at all, it is by interpreting events in the world with respect to our theory. If we can learn at all, it is by modifying and elaborating our theory. The theory fills our minds; we have no other resource.

THE THEORY OF THE WORLD IN THE HEAD

I use the term "theory" deliberately because the theory of the world that we have in our heads functions in exactly the same ways as a theory in science, and for exactly the same reasons. The main reasons can conveniently be summarized under the headings of "past, present, and future."

Relating Present to Past

For a start, scientists must have theories in order to summarize their past experience. Scientists are not interested in data—heaps of data merely clutter up their laboratories and interfere with the running of further experiments. Scientists instead strive for the best *summary* of their data, for statements of the regularities and invariances that seem to underlie experimental events. Scientists do not want to remember that on fifteen specific occasions the mixture of liquid A with powder B was followed by explosion C. Instead they want a rule, a summary, that the mixture of liquid A with powder B produces explosion C. Theories are integrated collections of such summary rules. In a far more general sense the human brain does not want to remember that on November 15 a chair was sat upon, on November 16 a chair was sat upon, on November 17 a chair was sat upon, and so forth; the brain wants to remember that chairs are for sitting on, a summary of experience. Everything we know about chairs, and about tables and houses and cars, about different kinds of food, about

different people's roles, about what can be done and everything that
happens and everything that is not likely to happen in the world is a
summary of experience, either direct experience or experience acquired through observation or communication. Generally we remember specific events only when they are exceptions to our summary
rules, or when they have some particularly dramatic or powerful or
emotional significance. Basically what we know about the world is a
summary of our experience in the world, and specific memories that
cannot be related to our summary, to our general rules, will make little
sense to us.

The brain seems so concerned with summarizing experience that it
even appears not to bother to memorize the details of anything it
already knows in general. We cannot remember specifically what we
had for breakfast yesterday morning because it was probably no
different from what we have for breakfast every morning. But if we had
eaten something unusual for breakfast, then we would have remembered it easily today.

The second reason that scientists must have theories is to make
sense of the world they are in, to interpret the new data coming in all
the time. Events that scientists cannot relate to their theories just
would not make sense to them. The scientists would be bewildered.
Theories protect scientists from bewilderment. It is for this protection
that we all need a theory in our heads embracing all of the world as we
perceive it. As I look around my world I distinguish a multiplicity of
meaningful objects that have all kinds of complicated relations to each
other and to me. But neither these objects nor their interrelations are
self-evident. A chair does not announce itself to me as a chair. I have to
recognize it as such. A chair does not *tell* me that I can sit on it, or put
my coat or books or feet upon it, or stand on it to reach a high shelf or
wedge it against a door I do not wish to be opened. All the order and
complexity I see in the world must reflect an order and complexity that
exists in my head. I can only make sense of the world in terms of what I
know already. Anything I could not relate to what I know already—to
my theory of the world in my head—would not make sense to me. I
would be bewildered.

When was the last time you were bewildered? The very fact that
bewilderment is such a rare condition for most of us, despite the
complexity of our lives, is a clear indication that the theory of the
world in our heads is at least as complex as the world we perceive
around us. The reason we are usually not aware of the theory is simply
that it works so well. Just as a fish takes water for granted until
deprived of it, so we become aware of our dependence on a theory to

make sense of the world only when the theory proves inadequate, when the world fails to make sense. When were you last bewildered by something that you heard or read? Our theory of the world seems ready to make sense of almost everything we are likely to experience in spoken and written language. A powerful theory indeed!

And yet, when was the last time you saw a bewildered baby? Infants have theories too, not as complex as those of adults, but then they have not had as much time to make their theories complex. But children's theories seem to work very well for the worlds they live in. Even the smallest children rarely seem confused or uncertain. The first time many children run into a situation they cannot possibly relate to anything they know already, when they are consistently bewildered, is when they arrive at school.

Prediction—The Theory in the Future

Our personal theory of the world, our summary of past experience, is more than a means of making sense of the present. Our theory is the arena of all our thought. The sober discipline of logical reasoning and the most exuberant flights of creative imagination all take place within its bounds. Scientists use their theories to make hypotheses that are the basis of future experiments, and our personal theory of the world is similarly employed to anticipate coming events. The third function of the theory is to predict the future.

Indeed our lives would be impossible, we would be afraid even to leave our beds in the morning, if we had no expectations about what each day might bring. We would be reluctant to walk out of a room if we could make no prediction about what might happen on the other side of the door. We live in a constant state of anticipation, but once again we are generally unaware of this because our theory functions so efficiently. When our predictions fail we are *surprised*.

This morning I had a visitor who was wearing brown shoes. That did not surprise me, I had predicted as much. But I would also not have been surprised if the shoes had been black. Evidently I had not predicted the specific color of the shoes. But my prediction was not without bounds; I would have been surprised if the visitor had been wearing purple shoes, or no shoes at all. On the other hand, if we had been on the beach, paddling in the shallow water, bare feet would not have surprised me and most kinds of shoes would have.

We drive through a town we have never visited before, yet nothing we see surprises us. There is nothing surprising about the buses and cars and pedestrians on the main street; they were predictable. But we did not predict that we might see anything—we would have been surprised to see camels or submarines in the main street. Not that there is anything very surprising or unpredictable about camels or submarines in themselves—we would not have been surprised to see camels if we had been visiting a zoo or to see submarines in a naval base. In other words, our predictions are very specific to situations. We do not predict that *anything* will happen, nor do we predict that something is *bound* to happen if it is only *likely* to happen (we are no more surprised by the absence of a bus than we are by the presence of one), and we predict that many things are unlikely to happen. Our predictions are remarkably precise, but once again that can only be because the theory of the world in our head is remarkably efficient. So much so that when our predictions fail we are surprised. When was the last time you were surprised?

But then, when was the last time you saw a baby who was surprised? It is not easy to surprise a baby. (I do not mean to startle a baby, with a physical shock, but to present an infant with a situation that is unexpected, unpredicted.) It is possible to surprise infants, but sometimes it takes a little ingenuity. Wave a rough papier-mâché mask of a human face—just a schematic nose with an eye on either side and a mouth beneath—in front of six-month-old babies and they will not give it a second look: "Ho hum, we have seen things like that before." At six months infants are not surprised by the appearance of a human face. But show the same infants the same papier-mâché face but with both eyes on the same side of the nose, and this time the infants will show all the symptoms of surprise. This is something they did not predict. Their response is not dissimilar to that of adults the first time they meet a painting by Picasso.

The Need for Prediction

Why should we predict? Why should we not expect anything all the time, and thus free ourselves from any possibility of surprise? I can think of three reasons. The first reason is that in the changing world in which we live, we are usually far more concerned with what is likely to happen in the near and distant future than we are with what is happening right now. We sometimes want to predict the future so that we can prevent or avoid it.

Every time we drive a car we are taking a trip through the future. We are never concerned with where the car is *now* (unless it happens to be stationary) but with where it will be at various times in advance of the present. I want to predict whether that truck at the intersection is likely to cross my path some time before it actually hits me. I must decide if my car and that pedestrian ahead will be trying to share the same spot on the road at the same time in the future. An important difference between a skilled driver and a learner is that the skilled driver is able to project the car into the future while the learner's mind is more closely anchored to where the car is now—when it is usually too late to avoid accidents. The same difference tends to distinguish skilled readers from beginners, or from anyone having difficulty with a particular piece of reading. In fluent reading the eye is always ahead of the words the brain is actually working on, checking for possible obstacles to a particular understanding. (This phenomenon is most easily demonstrated if the light is suddenly put out or the book closed while you are reading aloud. You continue reading a few words after you can no longer see, a clear indication that your eyes were ahead of your voice.) Readers concerned with the word directly in front of their nose are the ones who are having trouble predicting, and they are the ones who will suffer tunnel vision.

The second reason for prediction is that there is too much ambiguity in the world, too many ways of interpreting just about anything that confronts us. Unless we exclude some alternatives in advance we are likely to be overwhelmed with possibilities. The object that I see in front of me may be a chair, but if I am looking for somewhere to put my coat I do not want to be concerned with the fact that a chair is for sitting on or that it generally has four legs. What I see is related to what I am looking for, not to all the possibilities. I know where milk comes from, but that is not what I want to think of when I need a cool drink. Some authorities on language say that the meaning of a word is everything it makes us think of, but that is obviously nonsense in real life. The word *table* has many meanings—it can be a verb as well as a noun—but there is only one meaning that I am concerned with, that I predict, if someone tells me to put my books on the table. As I explained in the previous chapter, all the everyday words of our language have many meanings and often alternative grammatical functions, but in predicting the possible meanings a word is likely to have on a particular occasion, we are just not aware of the potential ambiguities.

The final reason for prediction is that there would otherwise be far too many alternatives to choose among. As I showed in Chapter 2, the brain requires time to make its decisions about what the eyes are looking at, and the time that it requires depends on the number of alternatives. It takes much longer to decide that we are looking at the letter *A* when it could be any one of the twenty-six letters of the alphabet than when we know that it is a vowel or that it is either *A* or *B*. The situation is fundamentally no different from when you have to distinguish your car in a parking lot. If there are too many alternatives confronting the eyes, then tunnel vision will be the consequence.

Now I can give a more specific explanation of what I have meant all this time by "prediction"—*prediction is the prior elimination of unlikely alternatives*. Prediction is not reckless guessing, nor is it a matter of taking a chance by betting on the most likely outcome. We do not go through life saying "Around the next corner I shall see a bus" or "The next word I read will be *rhinoceros*." We predict by disregarding unlikely alternatives. We use our theory of the world to tell us the most possible occurrences, and leave the brain to decide among those remaining alternatives until our uncertainty is reduced to zero. And we are so good at predicting only the most likely alternatives that we are rarely surprised.

Put more informally, prediction is a matter of asking questions. We do not look out of the window and wonder "What shall I see?"; we ask "Shall I see buses or cars or pedestrians?" and provided that what we are looking at falls within that limited range of alternatives our perception is effortless, efficient, and unsurprised. I do not ask "What is that object over there?" but "Can I put my books on it?" or whatever I want to do. We do not look at a page of print with no expectation about what we shall read next, instead we ask "What is the hero going to do; where is the villain going to hide; and will there be an explosion when liquid A is mixed with powder B?" And provided the answer lies within the expected range of alternatives—which it usually does if we are reading with comprehension—then we are not aware of any doubt or ambiguity.

The Relativity of Comprehension

Now at last I can say what I mean by "comprehension." Prediction is asking questions—and comprehension is getting these questions answered. As we read, as we listen to a speaker, as we go through life, we are constantly asking questions, and as long as these questions are answered, as long as we are left with no residual uncertainty, we comprehend. We do not comprehend how to repair a radio if we cannot answer our own question, "Which of these wires goes where?" We do not comprehend speakers of a foreign language if we cannot answer questions like "What are they trying to tell me?" And we do not comprehend a book or newspaper article if we cannot find answers to our own questions concerning information that we believe resides in the print.

You may observe that such a definition of comprehension is quite different from the way in which the word is used in school. Teachers often regard comprehension as the *result* of learning rather than the basis for making sense of anything. So-called comprehension tests are usually given after a book has been read, and as a consequence are more like tests of long-term memory. The fact that teachers frequently ask how to *measure* comprehension indicates that it is confused with learning. Comprehension is not a quantity, it is a state—a state of not having any unanswered questions.

Because comprehension is a state of zero uncertainty, there is, in the end, only one person who can say whether an individual comprehends something or not, and that is that particular individual. A test cannot tell me that I really did understand a book or a speaker if my feeling is that I did not. Of course there are some obvious clues that will indicate whether a person is not comprehending. If my eyes glaze over while you talk or my brow furrows deeply as I read, these are reasonable hints that all is not well with my comprehension. But the ultimate test must lie within the individual. This is the contention that so many teachers find so difficult to accept—that the best way of determining whether children can make sense of a book or a lesson from their own point of view is not to give them a test, but simply to ask "Did you understand?" (A child who will dissimulate is not making the reading a meaningful activity in any case.)

The very notion that comprehension is relative, that it depends on the questions that an individual happens to ask, is not one that all teachers leave unchallenged. They want to argue that you may not have understood a book however little uncertainty you are left with at the end. They will ask "But did you see that the police officer's failure to catch the speeding motorcyclist was really a symbol of ineluctable human helplessness in the face of manifest destiny?" And if you say "No, I just thought it was a jolly good thriller" they will tell you that you did not *really* comprehend what the story was about. But basically what they are saying is that you were not asking the kind of question they think you should have asked while reading the book, and that is another matter altogether. If there are particular questions a teacher thinks a student should ask then the teacher should announce the questions before the book is read, so that the student can truly predict and look for answers. But the teacher should be careful. Once again, too many questions, especially if the student does not really understand their point, can destroy comprehension altogether. (Sometimes a teacher will object: "If I tell students the questions in advance, they will not read any other part of the book." But isn't that what any intelligent person would do? When we look up a telephone number, do we read and try to memorize every other name and number in the directory?)

To summarize: the basis of comprehension is prediction and prediction is achieved by making use of what we already know about the world, by making use of the theory of the world in the head. There is no need to teach children to predict, it is a natural process, they have been doing it since they were born. Prediction is a natural part of living; without it we would have been overcome by the world's uncertainty and ambiguity long before we arrived at school.

There is also no need to instruct a child on the need to develop a theory of the world; this also is a natural part of being alive and growing up. From their earliest days infants summarize their past in order to make sense of the present and to predict the future. Without such a theory they would be constantly bewildered and frequently surprised. And neither bewilderment nor surprise are conditions that anyone is willing to tolerate for very long. It is a natural propensity of children to make their theories as extensive and efficient as possible.

How extensive is the theory of the world we have in our heads? To catalog this theory would be to catalog the world as we perceive it. All the order and complexity and predictability we detect in the world must reflect an order and complexity and ability to predict within our own brains. Of course, children's theories are not as complex as adults', but then no one's theory is ever complete. Perhaps I can distinguish more kinds of trees than you, although your theory is richer for distinguishing moths from butterflies, or for repairing car engines. The fact that a child may not be able to distinguish cats from dogs or the letter A from the letter B does not necessarily entail confusion or bewilderment, any more than I am usually confused or bewildered by my inability to distinguish moths from butterflies. These are just problems we have not yet got around to solving. A child's theory may be less differentiated than yours, but until you see a child who is constantly bewildered or surprised—and not just by what goes on in school, but by every aspect of life in general—you cannot say that the child does not know how to predict or to make sense of the world. Children know how to comprehend, provided they are in a situation that has the possibility of making sense to them.

LEARNING—DEVELOPING THE THEORY IN THE HEAD

Where has it come from, this fantastically complex yet precise and accurate theory of the world that we all have lodged in our brains?

Obviously we were not born with it. The ability to construct a theory of the world and to predict from it may be innate, but the actual contents of the theory, the specific detail underlying the order and structure that we come to perceive in the world, is not part of our birthright.

Equally obviously, very little of our theory can be attributed to instruction. Only a small part of what we know is actually *taught* to us. Teachers and other adults are given altogether too much credit for what we learn as children. But the debt we think we owe to formal instruction may be so deeply felt that a few illustrations may be required to show how exaggerated it is.

Consider for example what it is that we know that enables us to tell the difference between cats and dogs. What were we taught that has given us this skill? It is impossible to say. Just try to write a description of cats and dogs that would enable a being from outer space—or even a child who has never seen cats and dogs before—to tell the difference. Anything you might want to say about some dogs—that they have long tails or pointed ears or furry coats—will apply to some cats and not to some other dogs. (You cannot say that cats drink milk and dogs bark because how can you be sure that it is a cat drinking or a dog barking? Besides, the question is how we distinguish them on sight.) The fact is that the difference between cats and dogs cannot be put into language—it is *implicit* in our heads, knowledge that cannot be put into words. Nor can we communicate this knowledge by pointing to a particular part of cats and dogs and saying "That is where the difference lies."

Differences obviously exist between cats and dogs, but you cannot find and do not need language to distinguish them. Children without language can learn the difference between cats and dogs. Cats and dogs can tell the difference between cats and dogs. But if we cannot say what this difference is, how can we teach it to children? What we do, of course, is point out to children examples of the two kinds of animal. We say "That is a cat" or "There goes a dog." But pointing out examples does not teach children anything, it merely confronts them with the problem. In effect we say "There is something I call a cat. Now you find out why." The "teacher" sets the problem and leaves the child to discover the solution.

The same argument applies to just about everything we can distinguish in the world—to all the letters of the alphabet, to numbers, to chairs and tables, houses, foodstuffs, flowers, trees, utensils and toys, to every kind of animal, bird and fish, to every face, every car and plane and ship—thousands upon thousands of objects that we can recognize not only by sight but by other senses as well. And when did anyone tell us the rules? How often has anyone told us "Chairs can be recognized because they have four legs and a seat and possibly a back and arms"? (You can see how inadequate a description would be.) How often has anyone pointed out to us "A chair is something you can sit on" (as of course are many other objects that are not chairs)? Instead, somebody once said "There is a chair" and left us to decide not only how to recognize chairs on other occasions but also to discover what exactly the word "chair" means; how chairs are related to everything else in the world.

With reading we do not even need someone to set the problem in the first place. Reading at the same time presents both the problem and the possibility of its solution. Just by virtue of being a reader, every one of us has learned to recognize and understand thousands of words on sight. What we know about language is largely implicit, just like our knowledge of cats and dogs. So little of our knowledge of language is actually taught; we underestimate how much of language we have learned.

Ask most people how they pluralize words like "dog," "cat," and "judge" when they speak, and they will probably say they put an *s* on the end. But that is in writing; few people are aware of the /s/, /z/, and /iz/ sounds added in speech or of the rules that determine which is selected. It is not that we cannot put sounds together in other ways—there is a word "wince" but the plural of "win" is /winz/. And it is not that we are imitating, because children can correctly pluralize "words" they have never heard before—one wug, two /wugz/, one dak, two /daks/. There is a rule here—a rule we were never taught.

Our language is full of rules that we were never taught. You would think it odd if I told you I had a small wooden blue sailing boat, or a blue wooden small sailing boat. There is only one way to say what I want to say—I have a small blue wooden sailing boat, and just about every English speaker over the age of five would agree with me. Again, there is a rule—but it is not a rule that we can put into words. It is not a rule that we were taught.

I am not saying that there is nothing we are taught. We may be taught the rules of certain games just as we may be shown how to hold a fishing rod (although most of our skills come from practice rather than from direct instruction). Certainly we are taught that two times two is four and that Paris is the capital of France. But most of our theory of the world, including most of our knowledge of language, whether spoken or written, is not the kind of knowledge that can be put into words. It is more like the cat and dog kind of knowledge. Knowledge that no one can put into words is not knowledge that can be communicated by direct instruction.

How then—to repeat the original question—do we acquire and develop the theory of the world in the head? How does it become so complex and precise and efficient? There seems to be only one answer: by *experimentation*. Children develop their theories of the world in exactly the same way that scientists develop their theories—by conducting experiments.

Learning by Experiment

Scientists learn by conducting experiments designed specifically to put their theories to the test. Scientists do not experiment at random; they do not put liquid A and powder B together just to see what happens. Scientific experiments are planned with a deliberate end in view. Scientists conduct experiments to test *hypotheses*; they have certain expectations about how their experiments will turn out. They hypothesize that the mixture of liquid A with powder B will cause explosion C. The consequence of an experiment should never take a scientist by surprise.

The manner in which scientists elaborate and test theories is known as the experimental method and consists of just four simple steps: First, construct a hypothesis, a tentative development or modification of the theory; second, conduct an experiment to test the hypothesis; third, evaluate feedback, the results of the experiment; fourth, reject or tentatively accept the hypothesis accordingly.

There is one point to be underlined about this entire procedure; it begins and ends in the scientist's theory. At no point does the experimental method lose contact with what makes sense. Hypotheses arise out of theory, experiments are specific tests of hypotheses, feedback is specifically related to hypotheses (there can be no outcome that will take the experimenter by surprise). The consequence is a gain in knowledge, namely whether a particular development or elaboration of theory is warranted or not. Even in modifying their theories scientists never go beyond what can be explained by them. They never become enmeshed in nonsense.

Children learn in the same way as scientists, testing tentative modifications of their theories of the world through experiments.

Illustrations of the kind I am about to give have so impressed many students of children's learning that in some areas of research it has become customary to talk of "the child as an experimenter" or "the child as a scientist." But I do not think these analogies do sufficient credit to children. They suggest that children are precocious, raising the question of where children might get a specialized skill that among adults seems to be largely restricted to scientists. The analogy should go the other way. When scientists are conducting experiments they are behaving like children. Scientists—in the discipline of their professional activities—do deliberately and consciously what children do naturally, instinctively, and effortlessly. The "scientific method" is the natural way to learn, displayed by all of us in our early years. The problem as we get older is that we give up the basic requirement for learning by experiment—tentativeness. As we get older we become dogmatic (I tentatively propose). But in childhood the very basis of our learning is a willingness to look for evidence that might lead us to change our minds.

Children and Experiments

Let us look at some examples of learning through experimentation, beginning with the cat and dog problem. We have seen how pointing (or showing a picture) and saying "That is a cat" merely confronts children with the problem, which must then be solved. Suppose that from the example given, a child predicts—hypothesizes—that the rule for differentiating cats from dogs is that cats are always less than twelve inches high. The child can then test this hypothesis in experiments, by saying "There is a cat" or "What a nice cat" or "Hi cat" for any animal less than twelve inches high and "There is a dog" (or "That's not a cat") for any animal over twelve inches high. Relevant feedback is any reaction that tells the child whether the hypothesis was justified or not. If someone says "Yes, there's a pretty cat" or even makes no overt response at all, simply accepting the child's statement, then the child knows that the hypothesis has worked, on this occasion at least. The child's theory can be tentatively modified to include the rule that cats are animals under twelve inches in height. But if the feedback is negative—if someone says to the child "No, that's a dog" or even something as rude as "Think again, stupid," then the child knows that the hypothesis has failed. Another hypothesis must be tested. There is the scientific method at work on the cat and dog problem. Clearly more than one experiment will be required—it will take a lot of experience with cats and dogs before a child can be reasonably certain of having uncovered reliable differences between cats and dogs (whatever they may be). But the principle is always the same: stay with a hypothesis, and with your theory, for as long as it works; modify your theory, look for another hypothesis, whenever it fails.

Some critical points must be noted. The first is the importance of being able to ascertain what the problem is in the first place. A child will not learn to recognize cats simply by seeing cats; both cats and dogs (and other similar animals) must be seen in order for hypotheses about relevant differences to arise. Letters of the alphabet are learned by seeing them all, they are not learned one at a time. Second, hypotheses must be put to the test. A child cannot usually *tell* you the hypothesis—"I think that cats are always less than twelve inches high"—but must conduct experiments in order to get feedback that is relevant to the specific hypothesis being considered. Third, there must be a chance of being wrong. It is obvious that there is nothing to be learned if you know you are right; you know it already. But in addition, being wrong is more informative. Even though you are right, you might be right for the wrong reason (the animal under twelve inches high may be a cat, but that is not why it is a cat). When you are wrong you know your hypothesis is inadequate. We learn from our mistakes.

Finally, this entire process goes on automatically, instinctively, below the level of awareness. We are never aware of the hypotheses we test (if we were, then indeed we would be able to say what it is we know that enables us to tell the difference between cats and dogs). We are no more conscious of our hypotheses in learning than we are of the predictions that underlie our comprehension of language or of the world or of the theory of the world itself. But if you know what to look for, you can see this process of learning through hypothesis testing taking place with children. When does it take place? I think for young children there is only one answer: They are learning all the time.

Learning All the Time

Children who have just begun to talk often seem to make statements that are completely obvious. A child stands looking out of a window with you and says something like, "See big plane." You may even have pointed the plane out to the child. Why then should the child bother to make the statement? The answer is because the child is learning, conducting an experiment. In fact I can imagine no fewer than three experiments being conducted at the same time in that one simple situation.

In the first place the child is testing the hypothesis that the object you can both clearly see in the sky *is* a plane—that it is not a bird or cloud or something else as yet unidentified. When you say "Yes I see it," you are confirming that the object is a plane. Even silence is interpreted as positive feedback, since the child would expect you to make a "correction" if the hypothesis were in error. The second hypothesis that the child might be testing concerns the sounds of the language—that the name "plane" is the right name for the object, rather than "pwane," "prane," or anything else the child might say. Once again the child can assume that if you do not take the opportunity to correct, then there is nothing to be corrected. A test has been successfully conducted.

But the third hypothesis that the child may be testing is the most interesting of all. The child may be conducting a linguistic experiment, testing whether "See big plane" is an acceptable sentence in adult language.

Children do not learn to talk by imitating adults—not many adults say "See big plane" or the other baby talk we hear from children (unless the adults are imitating children). Nor do adults give children formal lessons in how to talk. Instead children use adults as *models;* children learn to talk like the adults around them by inventing their own words and rules which they modify whenever they have an opportunity—through experimentation—to come closer to adult language. One way in which children do this is by making statements in their own language for meanings that are perfectly obvious to adults and then by waiting for adults to put the statements into adult language so that they can make the comparison. For example, the child at the window making the very obvious remark "See big plane," is really asking "Is 'See big plane' a sentence in your language? Is that the way you would say it?"

It is in situations like this that parents, quite unwittingly, give children the information they need to develop language themselves. The child says "See big plane" and an adult says something like "Yes, I can see the big plane"—the adult provides an adult surface structure for the deep structure expressed in the child's own language, a basis for comparison. If the adult says nothing, or simply continues the conversation, the child assumes the hypothesis must be correct. But when adults correct—or more usually "expand" the child's utterance into adult language—they provide children with feedback that is relevant to their hypotheses. The expansions increase the meaningfulness of the situation. Children do not have to ask specific questions about grammar nor do adults have to teach children specific rules of grammar. Children move toward adult language by conducting experiments.

Sometimes these experiments seem to lead children into error. Children who have been successfully making statements like "Mummy came home" or "Daddy went out" will suddenly start saying "Mummy comed home" or "Daddy goed out." What is happening? Certainly the children are not imitating adults—adults do not say "goed" or "comed." Instead the children are trying out a rule that no one has explicitly taught them but they themselves have hypothesized. The past tense of *walk* is *walked*, the past tense of *kiss* is *kissed*, so it is a reasonable assumption that the past tense of *go* should be *goed* and the past tense of *come* should be *comed*. And so children produce works like *drinked* and *eated* and *seed* that they could never possibly have heard adults say. How do they straighten all this out? Not by asking specific questions like "Can you confirm the rule for constructing the past tense of regular verbs and give me a list of exceptions?" Instead, a child tests the hypothesis "The past tense of *go* follows the regular rule" by saying "Daddy goed." And the parent provides the relevant feedback by saying "Yes—Daddy *went*."

It is worthwhile to look closely at what goes on during these language-learning exchanges. The adult and the child are in effect speaking different languages but because they understand each other the child can compare their different ways of saying the same thing. Comprehension is at the core of the interaction; both adult and child can make sense of what is going on. Because adults know what a child means by statements like "See big plane" or even more outlandish utterances, they can provide models of how adult language would refer to the situation, leaving the learning to the child. The situation is basically no different from that in which adults say "There's a cat" and leave children to figure out the adults rules for recognizing cats.

The same principle of making sense of language by understanding the situation in which it is used applies in the other direction, as the child learns to *comprehend* adult speech. At the beginning of learning a language, infants must be able to understand sentences of a language before they can learn the language. I mean that children do not come to understand utterances like "Would you like a drink of juice?" or even the meaning of single words like "juice" by figuring out the language or by having someone tell them the rules. Children learn because initially they can hypothesize the meaning of a statement from the situation in which it is uttered—an adult is usually carrying or pointing to a drink of juice when a sentence like "Would you like a drink of juice?" is spoken. From such situations children can hypothesize that the next time someone mentions "juice" the drink that they recognize as juice will be involved. The situation provides the meaning and the utterance provides the evidence—that is all a child needs to construct hypotheses that can be tested on future occasions. Children do not learn language to make sense of words and sentences; they make sense of words and sentences to learn language.

Note here the intimate connection between comprehension and learning. Just as scientists' experiments never go beyond their theories—every stage of their experiments must make sense—so children must comprehend what they are doing all the time they are learning. Everything must make sense as they test their hypotheses—"If *drink of juice* refers to this glass of stuff in front of me, then a glass of it will be around the next time *drink of juice* is mentioned." Anything that bewilders a child will be ignored; there is nothing to be learned there. It is not nonsense that stimulates children to learn but the possibility of making sense; that is why children grow up speaking language and not imitating the noise of the vacuum cleaner.

Learning and comprehension cannot be separated. Comprehension is essential for learning and learning is the basis of comprehension. The process of comprehension and learning even seem to be fundamentally the same. In order to comprehend one must predict, in order to learn one must hypothesize, and both the prediction and the hypothesis come out of our theory of the world. The only difference is that predictions are based on something already part of our theory of the world—"Do I recognize a cat or a dog over there?"—while hypotheses are tentative modifications of the theory—"If I am right then that will be a cat over there." Predicting, hypothesizing, striving to comprehend, and striving to learn are going on all the time. They are as natural and continuous for a child as breathing.

Learning to Read by Reading

We learn to read by reading, by conducting experiments as we go along. We have built up a sight vocabulary of fifty thousand words—not by someone telling us fifty thousand times what a word is, but by hypothesizing the identity of new words that we meet in print and testing that our hypotheses make sense in the context. We saw in the previous chapter that the most preferred and efficient strategies for proficient readers when they come across a word that is unfamiliar are to skip or to predict from context and by analogy with other words. And we saw that these are also the most preferred and efficient strategies for children who are learning to read. Now we can see rather more clearly what this central process of "guessing" entails: not reckless conjecture but reasoned hypothesis-testing; not an act of blind despair but a precise and natural exercise of the human brain.

By conducting experiments as we read, we not only learn to recognize new words, we learn everything else to do with reading. We learn to make use of spelling-to-sound correspondences, not by memorizing the 166 rules and 45 exceptions of formal phonics instruction but by developing implicit procedures for distinguishing one word from another when the number of alternatives is limited to the most likely few. We learn not to rely too much on visual information in order to avoid the functional blindness of tunnel vision, and to avoid overburdening memory. We learn to sharpen and refine our ability to predict and hypothesize; we even learn to improve our own learning ability.

More remarkable still, perhaps, through reading we can add enormously to our understanding of all the words in our language. Put in everyday terms, we learn the meanings of words. When children learn spoken language the clues to meaning usually come from the surrounding situation, as in the juice example. But in written language the clues to meaning usually come from context. You may not know what the word *rundlet* means, but if you read that the seamen were carrying rundlets of rum on their shoulders from the stores to their ship you would probably guess that it was something like a small barrel—and you would be right.

Written language that makes sense is a basis for both the hypothesis and the test. Reading provides its own feedback. We make predictions about what we are about to read in order to comprehend, and we make hypotheses about what a particular word or passage is likely to be in order to learn. Our predictions and hypotheses come from what we understand about the passage already; and our feedback, the information that tells us whether we were right or wrong, comes from what we go on to read. If we have made a mistake we will probably find out about it—and that is the way we will learn. The sense of what we read not only supplies the basis for learning to read, it tells us when we are wrong. (You will notice that the preceding explanation depends on what we read having the possibility of making sense. We would never learn to read from something that was nonsense to us. The previous statements may sound so obvious you may wonder why I bothered to make them—until perhaps you reflect upon the way in which many children are expected to learn to read at school.)

We do not realize how much is learned by reading, not just about reading itself but about language and the world in general, because the learning is usually so effortless, so fluent. Learning to read takes place almost despite ourselves, and certainly despite our teachers—just as infants learn about language and the difference between cats and dogs.

The Cost of Not Learning

I have characterized learning as a continual and effortless process, as natural as breathing. A child does not have to be especially motivated or rewarded for learning, in fact the thrust to learn is so natural that being deprived of the opportunity to learn is aversive. Children will struggle to get out of situations where there is nothing to learn, just as they will struggle to escape from situations where breathing is difficult. Inability to learn is suffocating.

There is no need to worry that children who are not constantly driven and cajoled will "take the easy way out" and not learn. Young children who read the same book twenty times, even though they know the words by heart, are not avoiding more "challenging" material in order to avoid learning; they are still learning. It may not be until they know every word in a book in advance that they can get on with some of the more complex aspects of reading, such as testing hypotheses about meaning and learning to use as little visual information as possible.

Children will not stay in any situation in which there is nothing for them to learn. Everyone is equipped with a very efficient device to prevent wasting time in situations where there is nothing to learn. That device is called *boredom,* and boredom is something all children find intolerable. A child who is bored in class is not demonstrating ill will or inability or even sheer cussedness; boredom should convey just one very clear message for the teacher, that there is nothing in the particular situation that the child will learn.

Unfortunately there are two reasons why there might be nothing for a child to learn in a particular situation, and hence two causes of boredom. One reason children might have nothing to learn is very simple—they know it already. Children will not attend to anything they know already; they will be bored. But children exhibit the same symptoms of boredom not because they know something already, but because they cannot make sense of what they are expected to learn. Children cannot be made to attend to nonsense. It is a teacher's responsibility, not the pupil's, to make sure that what children are expected to learn has the possibility of making sense, not only in terms of what the children know already, but in terms of what they might want to know. Adults might see quite clearly that a certain exercise will improve a child's useful knowledge or skills, but unless the child can see some sense in the exercise, the instruction is a waste of time.

The Risk and Rewards of Learning

There is one other reason why children might turn their faces against learning, and that is its risk. In order to learn you must take a chance. The probability of learning is highest when there is a fifty-fifty chance of being wrong; if you are likely to be right nine times out of ten you will have the opportunity to learn only one time in ten. But children may become reluctant to learn because they are afraid of making a mistake. Consider the relative credit children are given in and out of school for being "correct" and for being "wrong."

There should be no need for special incentives to motivate a child to learn. Learning is a natural process. Children are motivated to learn whenever there is something relevant to them that they do not understand, whenever their theory of the world is inadequate to their needs or interests, whether as a summary of the past or as a basis for making sense of the present or predicting the future. Irrelevant inducements—bribing a child to attend—become necessary only when a child is confronted with nonsense, with something that does not make sense. And forcing a child to attend to nonsense is a pointless enterprise.

Nor does learning need to be rewarded. The final exquisite virtue of learning is that it provides its own reward. Learning is satisfying, as everyone knows. Deprivation of learning opportunities is boring and failure to learn is frustrating. If a child needs to be rewarded for learning—"reinforcement" is the technical term—then there is only one conclusion to be drawn: that the child does not see any sense in the learning in the first place.

Summary

The foundation of both learning and comprehension is the theory of the world that every individual has constructed and carries around in the head all the time. This theory is constantly tested and modified in all interactions with the world. It is the source of the predictions that enable us to make sense of events and of language, and the source of the hypotheses that when tested result in learning. If we cannot make sense of the world—if the situation confronting us cannot be related to our theory of the world—then there can be no comprehension and no learning. Learning takes place continually except in conditions of confusion, when there is no comprehension.

6

Readers and Reading

For five chapters I have talked very generally about how the eyes and brain work, about the functions of memory and the nature of language, about how we predict in order to comprehend and how we experiment in order to learn. These excursions were required before we could come to our central topic of reading because they all lie at the roots of reading. As I said at the beginning, there is nothing unique about reading; to understand reading it is necessary to understand broader topics. But now that we are at the threshold of a specific discussion of reading, there is a consolation: there is little new to be added. Most of what I now need to say about reading will be recapitulation, pulling together what I have said so far.

I shall begin by looking at what it is that proficient readers seem able to do. If we can identify the particular abilities that enable us to do the kinds of things that readers can do, then we shall have a basis for considering what it is that beginning readers must learn. A clear appreciation of what beginning readers need to learn will help us avoid the fallacy of confusing the nature of reading with the way reading is taught. One reason for the conventional oversimplification that reading is primarily the decoding of letters to sound must be that learning to decode to sound is what many of us mistakenly believe made us readers. It rarely crosses our mind that what our teachers did—or thought they were doing—in the classroom might have little to do with what we subsequently learned. And not many teachers are aware of the complexity and unreliability of the 166 rules and 45 exceptions (Chapter 4), let alone tell their students about this complexity and unreliability. What teachers actually accomplish may be very different from what they think they are doing. While trying to explain the sounds of letters, for example, they are often giving information and even practice relevant to the recognition of words. So in addition to analyzing reading before considering learning to read, I shall separate learning to read from all the complications of teaching reading. In fact, learning to read and reading instruction will be treated in separate chapters, as far as possible. For the present I shall begin with an analysis of reading, looking at what proficient readers like you and me are able to do.

What Is Reading?

There is no point in looking for a simple definition of "reading." "Reading" is no different from all the other common words in our language, it has a multiplicity of meanings. And since the meaning of the word on any particular occasion will depend largely on the context in which it occurs, we should not expect that a single definition for reading will be found, let alone one that will throw light on its mystery. One cannot even ask such a "straightforward" question as whether the process of reading necessarily entails comprehension.

If we recommend that a friend read a particular book we obviously intend the friend to comprehend it. It would be redundant to the point of rudeness to say we wanted the book to be read *and* comprehended. But on the other hand it would be quite reasonable for the friend to reply, "Well, I've already read the book but I couldn't comprehend it." We could not object that the friend had not read the book just because it was not comprehended. We might suggest reading the book again but it would not make sense to suggest going back to read it for the first time. So the word "reading" may sometimes entail "comprehension" and sometimes not, and any dispute about whether reading does or does not necessarily entail comprehension is a dispute about language, not about the nature of reading. To avoid endless semantic arguments—which are especially frustrating when we do realize that we are involved in one—we should stop looking for definitions of reading and consider instead what is involved in reading. Illustration, description, and analysis are after all what we usually want when we ask people to define their terms.

The Range of Reading

Consider all the different ways in which reading may take place, from the public recital of poetry to the private scrutiny of price lists and bus timetables. Making a list of all the different sorts of things that people might be called upon to read will perhaps sensitize us to the risk of oversimplification if reading is regarded too narrowly. I am not suggesting that there are many different kinds of reading, that we are doing something radically different when we read poetry rather than price lists. But looking at the range of reading will show the inadequacy of such "definitions" as "reading is the identification of written words" or "reading is the apprehension of the author's thoughts," neither of which for example would seem to apply to all the words we skip without identification on the way to the name we are trying to identify in a telephone directory. On the other hand, anything that we can discover that a wide range of reading situations have in common will surely give us a clue to central factors in reading. In education particularly, reading is often perceived extremely narrowly, in terms of *books*—and often only "great books" at that. To some, the sole purpose of reading would seem to be participation in the wisdom and delights of literature. (An emphasis that can put many individuals off serious reading for life.) The progression of children's reading ability is often judged in terms of the number of items of "children's literature" pupils have read. But there are other kinds of books apart from literature, apart from "stories" even, and apart from all the poetry and plays that are also found in print. There are all the textbooks and technical works that one might read for specific information, and many other books that are skimmed rather than studied, for reference rather than total immersion. There are books that no one would consider studying from cover to cover—dictionaries, directories, encyclopedias, timetables, catalogs, registers, bibliographies. And for all their variety, books constitute only a small part of our daily reading fare. Most of us read newspapers, with their headlines, news reports, picture captions, feature articles, sports scores, weather forecasts, market summaries, entertainment guides, and advertisements. The morning mail brings letters, forms, bills, magazines, journals, and more advertisements. There is print on television and print in the television guide. At the cinema there are the credits, at the theater the program. We read labels and menus, signs in stores and posters outside, traffic signs, street signs, destination signs, operating instructions, assembly directions, knitting patterns, recipes, computer programs, chemical formulas, and the formal expressions of logic and algebra. Some of us read special scripts, such as shorthand, or morse code, braille, or the sign language of the deaf.

Not everything we say we read is print. We read maps and wiring diagrams, compasses and meters, X rays, musical scores and dance steps. Our use of the word "read" extends into the abstract or metaphorical—we talk of reading tea leaves and palms, faces, the sky, the sea, the weather, and intentions. Is there anything that all these aspects of reading have in common?

Reading—Getting Questions Answered

Clearly one of the most common answers to the question of what is reading—the decoding of written words into sound—fails with respect to many of the examples I have given. If we utter or subvocalize a word at all while we are searching through a dictionary or telephone directory, it is the word we are looking for, not the words we are looking at. Besides, I have spent a large part of this book (particularly Chapter 4) trying to demonstrate that decoding to sound does not work. With dictionaries and directories it would also seem to be stretching a point to say that reading is "understanding the author's thoughts," a definition that similarly appears to have minimal relevance to reading street signs and package labels. Moreover definitions like "understanding print" or even "receiving communication" can hardly be said to *explain* reading; the problem still remains of how the reader understands the print or receives the communication. We are still left with the question of what the reader actually does.

A rather impressive-sounding technical definition of reading is "extracting information from text," which perhaps goes a little way toward putting reading into a clearer perspective but still ignores much of the problem. Obviously, getting information is something that is involved in all the different reading situations that I have listed—if you can read you can get information from directories and menus and street signs and record labels as well as from textbooks and novels—but there is a lot of information in much of this print that we do not get, for the very good reason that we do not want it. The telephone directory is bursting with information about the numbers of people we shall never want to call. The daily newspaper is replete with information from the publisher's name to the most esoteric small ad, deliberately ignored by most of us most of the time. Even when we read a novel we are unlikely to pay attention to all the information that is available in the print. As I tried to show in Chapter 2, undue concern with the "visual information" that lies in the surface structure of print can result only in interference with reading. The fluent readers in all aspects of reading are those who pay attention only to that information in the print that is most relevant to their purposes. It is indeed true that we extract information from print when we read—but very selectively. The basic skill of reading lies more in the nonvisual information that we supply from inside our head rather than in the visual information that bombards us from the print.

Any definition of reading should recognize the selective way in which we read all kinds of print, not striving mechanically to "extract" all the information the author or printer provides for us, but deliberately seeking just the information that we need, like finding a route between two places on a map. Information needed for what purpose? *To answer specific questions that we are asking.*

Here we have a conception of reading that does indeed cover all the different kinds of situations that I have listed—reading is asking questions of printed text. And reading with comprehension becomes a matter of getting your questions answered. "Getting your questions answered" is of course the way I tried to explain comprehension in the previous chapter. The only specific qualification to add for reading is that the information that answers the questions is found in printed or written text. You are able to read a telephone directory when you can find the answer to your question about the number of the particular person you want to call. You can read a menu when you can find the information that answers your question about the lunchtime special. You can read a novel or textbook when you are able to get sufficient information from the text to leave you with no unanswered questions, no confusion or bewilderment. When you look at a street sign you are asking "What street am I on?" or even more specifically "Am I on the street I am looking for?" Even metaphorical expressions like "reading faces" may be characterized as asking questions and finding answers.

This tendency to ask specific questions when we look at something extends far beyond the reading of print. As I explained when I discussed "prediction" as the basis upon which we make sense of the world, if we did not always have certain expectations or questions in mind, we would be constantly bewildered or surprised. Even when we look at a watch or clock we are likely to have a far more specific question in mind than "What time is it?" We want to know "Is it time to go home yet?" or "Am I late for my next appointment?" We do not so much want to know the time as whether we are on time. The next few times you see friends glance at a watch ask them what the time is. They will probably have to look at the watch again, for the simple reason they did not look to see the time, but whether or not it was some particular time they thought it might be. Because we often look at a clock to see if the hands have reached a particular position, digital clocks are not quite as convenient as the old-fashioned kind. A glance at a clock face will tell you if you are early or late, but with a digital timepiece you may have to make a calculation.

Readers' Questions

What questions do we ask when we read? To answer that question I would have to go once more through all the different reading situations listed a few pages ago. I would have to list the multiplicity of uses to which written language can be put. There is no simple answer because the questions readers ask depend precisely on the purpose of their reading in the first place. Except for rather obvious examples like looking up a particular telephone number or examining a menu or a sign, it is unlikely that any two people would ever in fact ask exactly the same questions of the same piece of text. That is why it would be unusual to get two identical interpretations—identical "comprehendings"—of the same novel or poem.

One of the most important skills of reading—which we certainly do not teach to any deliberate extent—is knowing the right kinds of questions to ask for different kinds of text. To read we must ask questions, *implicit* questions, not ones that we are aware of, just as we must ask implicit questions to comprehend spoken language. But the questions readers ask must vary with the material they are reading, which is why prior knowledge is so important. If we do not know the right kinds of question to ask of a math text or knitting pattern, then obviously we will not be able to read a math text or knitting pattern. And if we present children learning to read with material they cannot possibly ask questions of—because they find it boring, beyond their understanding, or simply because it is unequivocal nonsense in any case—then we should not be surprised if they cannot read. What questions could they be asking?

It is clearly not possible to be specific about the questions that readers might ask without going into an enormous amount of detail about all the different kinds of print that can be read, but it is possible to be quite specific about where they find the answers that they seek. Or at least, it is possible to be specific—even though a bit technical—about the nature of the visual information that readers look for in print in order to get their questions answered. To make my explanation easier—and in fact to make the crucial point about how reading is accomplished—I must now spend a few pages talking about how readers are able to find answers to specific questions about specific letters, words, and meanings. And I intend to talk about letters, words, and meanings in that order, simply for convenience in explication.

Despite the sequence of my discussion and the widespread belief that you need to recognize letters in order to identify words—and words to comprehend meanings—I shall try to demonstrate that reading actually works in the reverse direction. Normally we need to comprehend meanings in order to identify words and normally we try to identify words in order to identify letters. In fact we do not usually bother to go down the scale at all—we ignore letters if our aim is to identify words, and ignore words if we are reading to make sense. How is this trick accomplished? To explain all these rather unfamiliar ideas I must go one step at a time—in the reverse order—discussing first how readers identify letters.

The Identification of Letters

Here is a simple question. What is the letter in the box?

Here is a difficult question. How did you know? You cannot answer that you learned long ago that the letter was called "k"; such a response begs the question. I did not ask how you knew its name, but how you recognized in the first place the letter that you are naming. Before you can put a name to anything you must recognize it, you must "know what it looks like." What is it you know that enables you to recognize a letter of the alphabet? This is indeed a difficult question; in fact, scientists who study the visual system are quite uncertain about what precisely goes on when the eye and brain effortlessly perform their daily business of recognizing all the thousands of objects and forms that are familiar to us. But it seems reasonably clear that the feat is not accomplished by committing specific shapes or "pictures" of what we want to recognize to memory. We do not have a picture book or filing cabinet of letter shapes in the brain to which we refer whenever we want to say what a letter is. You did not recognize the *k* in the box by comparing it with a set of conveniently labeled pictures or representations of the alphabet in the mind.

One reason that it is unlikely that we learn to recognize the alphabet by memorizing the shapes of letters is that letters come in so many shapes and sizes:

k K k k k K K k k k K K K K K k

I am sure there were one or two *k*'s in the previous sequence that you had never seen before in that identical form, and that were therefore different from any "picture" you might have in your memory. The situation is quite general—we can identify cats and dogs we have never previously seen just as we can recognize faces and cars from angles at which we have never seen them before.

We may not have given much thought to the question of how letters of the alphabet—or cats and dogs, people and cars—are recognized, and the question of how we do so may itself sound a bit odd. But our lack of curiosity is because we are so good at recognizing familiar objects and forms; visual recognition is one of those incredibly complex skills for which we give the brain little credit because both the learning and the performance of the skills are usually accomplished without strain or awareness. But it is important for anyone concerned with reading to understand that we do not learn to recognize letters or anything else simply by "memorizing" shapes, even if many views about how reading should be taught seem to be based on just that assumption.

The best simple answer to the question of how you were able to recognize the letter k in the previous example is that you decided it could not be one of the other twenty-five letters of the alphabet. In other words, what you have learned is how to distinguish each letter of the alphabet from the others. You have knowledge about what constitute *significant differences* among the letters of the alphabet. (Perhaps you can begin to see why different views of how letters are learned make a difference to instruction. The "picture memorizing" view might seem to suggest that a child should be taught letters of the alphabet one at a time, given lots of practice until a is learned and then moving on to b, and so forth. But the view I am outlining suggests that in order to learn how to identify any letter you must see what the alternatives are. Children cannot even begin to learn to recognize a until they can compare it with every letter that is not a.)

The important word in the explanation that letters are recognized on the basis of significant differences is "significant." There are differences between k and K—the two letters clearly do not look absolutely alike—but these differences are not significant because we normally want to treat the two letters as the same, namely as "k." The letters k and h also do not look alike, but this time there must be differences that are significant because the two letters cannot be treated as if they are the same. So the problem for anyone trying to learn to distinguish k from h is to discover the differences that are significant—the "differences that make a difference." Researchers sometimes refer to these significant differences as *distinctive features*. Presumably one of the distinctive features of A, for example, as compared with H, is that it comes to a point on top. A distinctive feature of O as compared with C must have something to do with the closure of a circle. However, it is not possible to be very specific about what actually constitutes the set of distinctive features of letters (or of anything else) for the very good reason that we do not know enough in detail about how the visual system works. Scientists cannot say precisely what the eye looks for. And in any case, another good reason for not speculating too much about distinctive features is that some teachers might be tempted to try to teach these features to children, a concern that is certainly unnecessary and possibly distracting.

Incidentally, learning to make distinctions on the basis of significant differences among alternatives is again not a process unique to reading; it applies to everything else we can distinguish, including our familiar example of cats and dogs. We are able to identify a cat, from a mere glimpse from the other side of the street, even when it is a cat that we have never seen before, because we have knowledge that enables us to distinguish cats from dogs and from other four-legged animals that are not cats. (Having four legs is not a distinctive feature of cats compared with dogs, although it is of course a distinctive feature of both cats and dogs as compared with snakes and goldfish.) Two points emerge from the analogy of cat and dog recognition with recognition of letters of the alphabet. The first is that we are not aware of all the distinctive features that enable us to distinguish different things—this is *implicit* knowledge; we clearly have it in our brains, but it is not knowledge that we can put into words. The second point is that what constitutes a distinctive feature is relative to the distinctions we want to make. What enables me to distinguish a dog from a cat may not enable me to distinguish a dog from a wolf.

To say that our ability to recognize individual letters is based on a knowledge of distinctive features rather than on an internalized set of pictures is another way of saying that what we have learned is *rules*, or procedures, for distinguishing letters of the alphabet. We have acquired a set of rules that enables us to test whether a particular letter is *k* or some other letter of the alphabet. We shall soon be very concerned with how these rules are learned, but for the moment I want to illustrate the way we employ rules or distinctive features to distinguish letters. The discussion will bring together a lot of the research evidence I presented earlier in the book, and will provide a basis for explaining how we can recognize words and comprehend meanings so fluently.

There are several lines of evidence supporting the distinctive features view, for example the fact that even if we cannot see enough to identify a letter for certain, we can often have a good idea of what it is not. We may confuse the letter *a* with *e* or *s* but never with *k*, while *m* might be confused with *w* but not with *p*. This suggests that even a glimpse of part of a letter—discrimination of a few distinctive features—can help to eliminate some alternatives.

The ease with which we can identify any letter depends on the number of alternatives that we think the letter might be. It is easier to recognize *a* if we know in advance that it is a vowel than if we think it could be any one of the twenty-six letters of the alphabet. We can recognize the letter quicker, or when it is smaller or further away, with less chance of error. This fact, that ease of recognition does not simply depend on how big or clearly printed the letter is, but also on the uncertainty of the reader, is based upon a wealth of experimental evidence; nevertheless it comes as something of a surprise. Common sense might tell us that either we can see a letter or we can not. Just as common sense might tell us that either we have learned to recognize a letter or we have not. But, in fact, the ease with which we can both learn and identify a letter depends on the number of alternatives. The fewer the alternatives, the less evidence we need to make a decision. This is a universal phenomenon, as I pointed out in the last chapter when talking about perception and comprehension generally. The evidence you require to identify a letter—the number of distinctive features you need to discriminate—depends on how many different letters you think it could possibly be.

This fact that individual letters can be recognized in a poorer light, or from a greater distance, when some limitation is placed on the number of alternatives that the letter might be can only be explained by the distinctive feature theory. If letter recognition were a matter of matching a shape with a picture in the head, what would it matter if there were two alternatives or two hundred? Either you would see a letter or you would not, and clues would not help. The distinctive feature theory helps to account for the important demonstration we considered at some length in Chapter 2, when we saw that in one second of reading the visual system could deal with only four or five letters if the letters were selected at random:

W K H M Y

but twice as many if the letters were arranged into words:

F U R Y   H O R S E S

When letters are printed at random the probability of each letter is one in twenty-six and a good deal of distinctive feature information is required to make a decision. But when letters are organized into words the relative probability of each letter is reduced to an average of about one in eight. (If you see the letter *q* in an English word you need not discriminate *any* distinctive features to tell you what the next letter will be. After *qu* there are only five alternatives.)

In Chapter 2 I talked about the trade-off between visual and nonvisual information in reading, explaining that the more nonvisual information you have behind the eyeballs, the less visual information from the page your brain has to handle. It is the nonvisual information, or what you know already about how letters occur in words, that reduces alternatives for you in advance; the distinctive features available in the letters on the page constitute the visual information that enables you to decide among the remaining alternatives. You would not be able to make use of your prior knowledge and identify two or more times the letters in a single glance when they occur in predictable sequences unless you were able to make use of the identifications of units of information much smaller than a single letter; distinctive features, in other words.

All this explanation, incidentally, should now help you to realize that the test I gave when I asked if you could identify the *k* in the box was the most difficult I could devise without making the actual letter more difficult to discriminate. I could have made the task much easier by telling you that the letter was in the first half of the alphabet, or that it was either *j*, *k*, *l*, or *m*, for example. Of course, we are not usually aware of the gain in time or clarity when the number of alternatives that a letter might be is reduced, but that is because in situations of the kind I have described we normally have more than enough time and information to make our decision. It is only on the rare occasions when we might be called upon to read through lists of random letters rapidly—or if we are school children required to identify a lot of nonsense written on a board or in a book—that the difficulty of identifying letters on the basis of visual information can make itself felt.

All this is also evidence that reading is not a passive process that begins with the print on the page and ends with a reaction in the brain. Even as simple a matter as recognizing letters of the alphabet begins with a question that we are asking—the predicted range of alternatives—and ends with a search for an answer on the page. The question is always in terms of the alternatives we are considering—which of the twenty-six letters of the alphabet is this, or which vowel is it, or is it the letter *j*, *k*, *l*, or *m*? And the answer is found in the marks on the page, the distinctive features that enable us to make our decisions about what we are looking at. (Sometimes we can look at exactly the same distinctive features and get quite different answers, depending on the question we happen to be asking. If we are asking a question about letters, then the features in Ol will be read as letters, as in the name Oliver. But if our question is about numbers then the same features will give us a numerical answer as in the sequence 01234).

The Identification of Words

Here is another easy question. What is the word in the box?

HOUSE

Here is another difficult question. How did you know? As I explained at the beginning of Chapter 4, you certainly did not recognize the word by sounding it out—by putting together the sounds of individual letters. If I could have timed you we would have found that it takes little longer to put a name to the entire word than it would to utter the sound of a single letter. Besides, I am sure you did not run through the eleven different ways of pronouncing *HO* before you said what the word was. Nor did you recognize the word on the basis of its spelling—you did not read the letters "h," "o," "u," "s," "e" and refer to some kind of internal dictionary to ascertain that those letters spelled the word "house." If you could read the word *house* at all then you would have recognized it at once, without any figuring it out through phonics or spelling. You would have recognized the word as a unit, just as you earlier recognized the letter *k* as a unit, and indeed just as you would recognize a real house or a picture of a house as a unit, not a bit at a time. In other words, when we read a word we do not read letters at all.

In many written languages, of course, there are no letters in any case. Chinese children learn that 家 is the written symbol for house—they cannot sound it out. For fluent readers of English like you and me the fact that the words of our written language are made up of letters is largely irrelevant—we recognize words in the same way that fluent Chinese readers recognize the words of their nonalphabetic written language, as self-contained and immediately recognizable units.

In Chapter 4, you may recall, I made a distinction between two aspects of learning to identify words—finding out the "name" of the word and remembering how to recognize on future occasions the printed marks to which the name should be attached. Phonics was only one way—a relatively inefficient way—of finding out the name of unfamiliar words and had nothing to do with the way words were normally recognized. Now we can examine further how words are recognized so that their names and possible meanings can be related to the visual information. The answer is that words are recognized in exactly the same way that cats, dogs, cars, faces, and letters of the alphabet are recognized. Words are recognized on the basis of significant differences among alternatives, on the basis of distinctive features.

We learn to recognize words by learning to distinguish them from each other. Exactly the same arguments apply to the recognition of words that I have just used to support the distinctive theory for the recognition of letters. Asking you—or a child—to recognize a word in isolation is the hardest word recognition task that can be given. The word would have been much easier for you to recognize—and you would have been more confident that you were right—if I had told you that it was a building or if I had put it into a sentence. When words are in a meaningful context, or when we have a pretty good idea of what they are likely to be in the first place, we can see them much quicker and over a much greater distance than if we have no prior expectations at all.

As with letters, it is not simply a case of either we see a word or we do not—any more than it is a case of either we have learned a word or we have not. The ease with which we recognize words depends on the number of alternatives we think there are. The more alternatives, the more information or distinctive features we need to discriminate. In a meaningful sequence like "I like e — — s and b — — — n for breakfast," we need see only small parts of a word to be able to recognize it. And these small parts are not letters; the distinctive features of words are clearly smaller than letters because an entire word can be recognized in the time it takes to identify a single letter. Obviously we do not spend as much time on any of the letters in a word as we would spend on the letters in isolation. Letters can be mutilated so much that it is impossible to identify them by themselves, yet they are recognizable in words.

The fact that the number of distinctive features required to identify a word depends on the number of alternatives helps to explain another aspect of the Chapter 2 demonstration that I have already discussed. We can see only two unrelated words—like FURY HORSES—if each word could be one of many thousands of alternatives. But when the number of alternatives is limited, because the words are grammatical and make sense, we can see twice as much—EARLY FROSTS HARM THE CROPS.

What are the distinctive features of words? Obviously they are the same as the distinctive features of letters since words are made up of letters, with perhaps one or two additional features like relative length and the relative position. If you know a word is either *cat* or *cucumber*, length alone will identify it for you. The distinctive features of words like the distinctive features of letters must lie in the ink marks on the page. Sometimes—when we want to identify letters—we look at those ink marks, the "visual information" of print, and see letters. Sometimes—when we want to identify words—we look at the ink marks and see words. In other words, what we see, whether letters or words, depends on the *question* we are asking. The answer always lies in the same source of information, the distinctive features in the ink marks on the page, but whether we see letters or words depends on what we are looking for, just as whether we see O1 as numbers or letters depends on what we expect. We can see letters without seeing words, as you would if I asked you to read the letters in the word *house* backwards. But we can also see words without seeing letters. You do not have to read "h" "o" "u" "s" "e" in order to read the word *house*. In fact it is not possible to do the two things at the same time; you cannot see both letters and words in the same place at the same time any more than you can see the two faces and the vase at the same time in the following picture. The brain can only handle the answer to one question at a time. Attention to the meaning of words, for example, can make you oblivious to their spelling, as any proofreader knows.

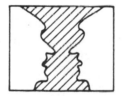

Now perhaps you can see why I wanted to talk about letter recognition before talking about word recognition—because it is simpler to explain the notion of distinctive features with reference to letters. But now I hope you also see why I stressed that I was putting letter recognition first simply for convenience, that I did not want you to think that letter recognition was a necessary prerequisite for word recognition, either in learning or performing the recognition skill. When you recognize words that are familiar to you, you need pay no attention to letters at all. We only attend to letters when we fail to recognize whole words, and unless we have a fairly reasonable idea of what a word might be, using the letters to sound it out will still do little to help. As I pointed out in the previous chapter, there are easier ways of identifying unfamiliar words.

Making Sense of Text

The idea that both letters and words are recognized in the same way, through the discrimination of distinctive features that are elements of written language smaller even than a letter, does not usually cause too much difficulty. Although our immediate intuitions may be to the contrary, it is not hard to grasp that if individual letters are recognized on the basis of distinctive features then words themselves should be distinguishable from each other by virtue of the same features, without the intervening necessity to identify letters. But the next step will probably be a little harder to grasp. *When we identify meaning in text, it is not necessary to identify individual words.* We can make sense of text directly from the distinctive features of the print, from those same distinctive features in the ink marks on the page that we can employ for the recognition of letters and words.

We may *think* we see words we read, but there are several reasons for this misconception. For a start, this is a case where we cannot trust our own senses. The mere circumstance of wondering whether in fact we identify words when we read will ensure that we are indeed aware of recognizing words as we read—for as long as we ask ourselves that question. It is impossible to observe oneself reading to see if we are aware of words without in fact being aware of words (just as we may think we "subvocalize"—or read "silently to ourselves"—every time we read because whenever we listen for this inner voice we subvocalize). But the fact that we cannot avoid focusing our attention on words if we look to see if we are attending to words does not mean that we normally read by identifying words. It would be impossible to read normally—that is, to make sense of the print—and at the same time attend to the individual words. Perhaps at some point during the last few sentences you did in fact wonder whether you were aware of individual words as you read. And if for a while you became aware of words I am confident that at least one and probably both of the following things happened to you. You slowed down tremendously in order to read-one-word-at-a-time, and for a while you lost track of meaning. I do not want to assert that you cannot recognize individual words when you read; obviously you can. But the recognition of individual words is not necessary for comprehension, and conversely comprehension is often necessary if you want to identify individual words.

The fact that words are so obviously there on the page in front of us is no justification for asserting that we attend to them as words, any more than the fact that words are made up of letters entails that we identify every letter. Obviously we *look at* words, in the same sense that we look at the paper they are printed on, but we need be no more *aware* of the words than we are of the paper if we are concerned with meaning. The moment we pay attention to such irrelevant details as the paper or the print, we risk losing concentration upon the sense of what we are reading.

The matter is further complicated because letters and words—or their surface structures—are so self-evident, but the very notion of a "meaning" is vague and intangible. You cannot point to particular units of written language and say "There is one meaning" in the same way that you can point and say "There is one word" or one letter. Furthermore, there is the weight of so much conventional opinion for the opposite point of view. The response of many teachers when they first understand and grasp the implications of what I am about to explain is "Why were we never told this before, in our training?" I shall offer an answer to that question toward the end of this book.

At the moment I want to present the evidence that the apprehension of meaning can precede the identification of individual words, and then try to show that normal reading *demands* comprehension prior to and even without the identification of words. These may be the hardest ideas to grasp in this book, but they are the most crucial.

Since words are hard to ignore when one is especially thinking about them, it is difficult—but not impossible—to demonstrate comprehension of a word's meaning without actual identification of the word. So generally the technique employed by researchers to demonstrate the pre-eminence of meaning is to show that sequences of words are identified faster if they are meaningful than if they are not. For an example we can turn once again to the demonstration in Chapter 2 that two unrelated words would be read in a single second:

FURY   HORSES

but that more than twice as many can be read in the same time if the words make sense:

EARLY FROSTS HARM THE CROPS

The argument is that the second sequence could not have been identified a word at a time in the same way that FURY HORSES was, otherwise no more than two words of the second sequence would have been identified. Something about the meaningfulness of the entire second sequence facilitated the identification of the individual words, so something about the meaning must have been comprehended before any of the words were identified. And the reason the meaningfulness could have this facilitating effect was also given in Chapter 2: when words are in meaningful sequences the number of alternatives is very much smaller. The average probability of each word in meaningful sequences is about one in two hundred rather than one in many thousands for isolated, random words.

Whether or not we see a word depends on how many alternatives there are. The fewer alternatives, the fewer distinctive features we need to discriminate. Meaningfulness cuts down on the number of alternatives, and thus we are able to make use of meaning to reduce how much we need look at the distinctive features that constitute a word. We can even begin to get clues about the meaning of a phrase before there has been time to identify more than one or two words, as in the example just given. The effect of meaningfulness is extremely powerful. It is not difficult to demonstrate that it doubles the rate at which we can read, which is another way of saying that the eye requires only half the distinctive feature information for each word if the words make sense. You can demonstrate this to yourself by seeing how much slower you are at reading a sentence that is written backwards: Discriminate to need we features distinctive fewer the, alternatives fewer the.

If you do try to read nonsense at your normal reading speed you will find you get more words wrong. Not that errors are an unusual occurrence in reading. Despite the emphasis placed on accuracy in schools, everyone makes mistakes while reading, even professional readers like actors and broadcasters, unless they have had a lot of rehearsal to commit the actual words to memory. But the interesting thing about the errors that fluent readers make is that the errors usually make sense—the readers do not read the exact words, but they usually get the meaning right. They might read something like "Johnny hadn't got a ticket" when the text actually says "Johnny had no ticket" but not something like "Johnny had a ticket," which looks more like the text but has a different meaning. Children who are on the way to becoming skillful readers make a lot of mistakes that make sense, reading "Johnny told me . . . " rather than "Johnny said . . . ," suggesting that they have discovered they should not spend too much time looking at particular words. Children who are not progressing so well tend to look at words more closely and to make errors that perhaps are less extreme in terms of visual similarity—"Johnny sand . . ." instead of "Johnny said . . ."—but that make no sense. Good readers when they do make a mistake that turns out not to make sense usually go back and correct themselves, because they are attending to meaning. But children aiming for individual word accuracy do not correct their mistakes since they cannot become aware of them—they are not following the sense. (Of course, if what the children are reading is nonsense in any case the good readers will be forced to read just like the bad.)

An ingenious demonstration that people read for meaning with complete disregard for the particular words they are looking at has been provided by studies of fluent bilingual adults reading text that changed every couple of words from English to French—sentences like *His horse, suivi de two dogs, faisait resonner the earth.* Not only could such readers subsequently not remember which parts of the text were in English or French—and some even said they did not notice that the text was in two languages—but often they read the English words in French or vice versa. They would read, without correcting themselves, phrases like *two dogs* as "deux chiens," conserving the meaning, of course, but completely ignoring the actual evidence of their eyes.

Even more dramatic evidence that meaning can be independent of the literal word comes from brain-injured patients who seem to have lost precise word recognition skills but who can nevertheless grasp the general meaning of familiar words. Some have been reported to have "read" the isolated word *ill* as "sick," *city* as "town," and *ancient* as "historic." This phenomenon is not dissimilar to the difficulties of other aphasic patients who cannot identify a pair of scissors by name but who can say they are "for cutting." They are able to recognize the sense of something without being able to put an exact name to it.

But then, there is no good reason to "say" what a written word is, either aloud or silently, in order to grasp its meaning. We get the meaning of HOUSE, for example, directly from the printed marks and then if necessary say the word, just as we recognize a real house before we say "There is a house." We recognize a face—we comprehend its "meaning" to us—before we put a name to it. Why should it be surprising that we can comprehend a written word's meaning before we put a name to the word? For some words we cannot even put a name to them until we know their meaning (should read be pronounced "reed" or "red"?). And for many other words, like *their* and *there*, saying the word will not give us the meaning.

A final illustration comes from experiments in which participants are required to read through lists of words in order to identify a particular "target"—for example, going down a list of thirty or forty unrelated five-letter words looking for the word *maple.* The task is not

unlike going down the page of a telephone directory for a particular
name. In both cases you find that relatively little time is taken in getting to the word you are looking for—you are paying only minimal
attention to the words you do not want. In fact you can usually not say
very much about the words that you "read" that were *not* the word
you were looking for because in fact it is not necessary to identify a
word to say what it is not. Far fewer distinctive features are required
for a decision that a word is not something than to confirm what it is.
None of this is surprising, perhaps, except that in the experimental
situation it has been shown that it takes no longer to find the target
word when readers are simply told "It is a kind of tree" than when they
are told specifically that the word is *maple*. They can read for the
general meaning just as easily as they can for the specific word. In fact
the tendency to concentrate on meaning rather than on the specific
word can interfere with reading in some circumstances. It takes longer
to find the exact word *maple* when it is hidden among a lot of other tree
names than when it is among words with a variety of different meanings.

Finally, comprehension must precede the identification of individual words for the simple reason, explained in the last chapter, that
words taken in isolation, or one at a time, are essentially meaningless.
You cannot tell the part of speech of common words like *chair, table,
house, narrow, empty, waste*, let alone their meaning, unless you have
some idea of what you are reading about. Unless, in other words,
comprehension is preceding the actual words.

But if comprehension is necessary before words can be identified,
and if the purpose of reading is to make sense of the text, then there is
often no point in identifying the individual words at all. Meaningful
language is *transparent*: we look through the words for the meaning
beyond.

The Strategies of Reading

To summarize the preceding section: we can read for meaning
without the prior identification of individual words, just as we can
identify words without the prior identification of the individual letters.
Of course, if we cannot achieve meaning directly then we may try to
work it out from the individual words, just as we may try to identify an
unfamiliar word from its individual letters. But both alternatives
are largely impractical; they leave too much uncertainty. It is difficult to identify an unfamiliar word on the basis of its component
letters because of the complexity and unreliability of phonic rules,

and it is almost impossible to work out the sense of a difficult sentence from the meanings of its component words because of all the alternative meanings that individual words can have. In both cases what makes meanings and individual words become transparent to us is *context*, which means the general sense in which the difficult element is embedded. Provided that what we are trying to read has the possibility of making sense to us, the parts that are unfamiliar can usually be deciphered because of all the other clues that are available. But if we are reading something that is largely nonsense then the identification of unfamiliar words is likely to be difficult from two perspectives. Neither the individual letters nor the text in general are likely to provide sufficient information to make word identification possible. And in any case the entire enterprise is pointless because even if individual words are identified they are unlikely to give sufficient clues to the meaning as a whole.

Reading directly for meaning, then, becomes the best strategy for reading; not a consequence of reading words and letters, but an alternative. It is true that fluent readers can generally do all three things—identify letters, identify words, and comprehend meanings. But these are independent aspects of reading; readers cannot and do not accomplish them at the same time. We read words without reading letters, and read meanings without reading words. In each case we are looking at the same thing—the distinctive features that are embedded in the text—but asking a different question. We can look at the text and ask questions about letters, in which case we shall require a relatively concentrated amount of visual information and see very little. Or we can look at the text and ask questions about words, in which case we shall see a little bit more but probably not enough to make sense of what we are trying to read. Or we can look at text and ask questions about meaning, in which case we shall not be aware of individual words but we shall have the best chance of reading fluently and meaningfully. Paradoxically enough, because we are concentrating on meaning we shall have the best chance of getting individual words right, should we be reading aloud.

What kinds of questions do we ask if we are reading for meaning? For specific letters or words the answer is easy, but it would be pointless to attempt anything like an exhaustive list of all possible meanings. The specific questions a particular reader might ask at a particular time depend on what is read and the reasons for reading it. Reasons for reading can vary at least as much as all the different kinds of reading situations that I outlined at the beginning of this chapter. However, by taking the discussion back to some of the different reading situations I can once more illustrate that comprehension in reading is a matter of asking and getting answers to questions.

Consider reading a menu. How often do we read a menu from top to bottom, left to right, noting every word, with no expectation of what we are likely to see and no particular interest in anything we might be likely to find out? We read menus with a purpose and examine them—we ask our questions—selectively. We might ask "What's on for dessert?" or even more specifically "Is there apple pie?" and possibly our next question is "How much?" We know what information we want and we have a pretty good idea of where to look for it. We can predict the alternatives from which words and phrases on the menu are likely to be drawn and we could certainly predict many thousands of words most unlikely to occur. And indeed, we would be most surprised if any of these unlikely and therefore unpredicted words occurred. Since we have only a few alternatives in our mind—thanks to all the nonvisual information we bring to reading menus—very little visual information is required from the distinctive features in the print to give us our answers. A glance usually tells us what we want to know. (If we spend a lot of time looking at a menu it is not because it takes a long time to read it but because we cannot make up our minds.) There is usually no tunnel vision in reading a menu because we are reading it for sense, not at the letter-by-letter level or as if it consisted of unpredictable and unrelated words.

Suppose I am looking at a telephone directory to find the number of my friend Jack Jones. My first question as my eye runs down each column is "Jones?" (meaning "Is this word I am focusing on Jones?"). I need so little visual information to answer this question that I can run my eyes down columns of names at the rate of thousands of lines a minute. When I find myself among the Joneses my eye moves slightly to the right and my next question is "Jack?," followed by a check of middle initials and addresses. And when I find the Jones I want the critical question becomes "What is the number?"—the answer to which is the only information I commit to memory. We do not read telephone directories as if they were menus—not if we are competent readers and comprehend what we are doing. The *process* of reading is basically the same in both instances—predicting and getting the answer to questions—but the situations differ because of the different questions that we ask. As I have said before, if we do not know what questions to ask then we do not comprehend. Hence the difficulty I would have trying to find a number in a Tokyo telephone directory.

In reading a knitting pattern, or a recipe, or instructions for assembling a bicycle, a preliminary question must often be "Where am I now?" (meaning "Where is the place that I have got to so far?"—and you will note that this quite specific question is not unlike the search for the name we want in a telephone directory or for a wanted word in a dictionary). The next question, to phrase it very loosely, is something like "What should I do now?," but if we have any understanding of what we are doing it is likely to be much more specific, something like "Should I add the eggs now or the butter?" or "Do I attach the ring-bolt before the switch assembly?" If we do not understand what we are doing, if we have no expectation of what the next step is likely to be, then we are unlikely to understand the instructions, or even to be able to find our place in them. "What should I do now?" questions may sound very vague, but in fact for comprehension to take place there has to be a limited range of alternatives, both to ease the information-processing burden on the brain and to protect us from surprise and bewilderment.

When we come to consider more complex texts than menus and telephone directories—for example newspaper and magazine articles, technical reports, and novels—it is not so easy even to illustrate what the questions might be. Many questions would differ from one novel to another, obviously depending on the characters and the plot; other questions would differ from one part to another of the same novel. Some questions may persist through long sections of a book—"Which suspect is the murderer?"—while others may not extend beyond a sentence—"Is the poison victim dead? (You get through a novel by having current questions answered and moving on to the next question. If at any time you fail to find an answer that you need you are likely to be confused and uncomprehending, but if you are left with no questions to ask you will either be bewildered or bored.)

Possibly there are some basic questions that are part of our comprehension of all novels, but that issue seems to me part of a theory of literature, beyond any analysis of the basic processes of reading. Questions that some specialists think readers should ask about such recondite matters as style and technique—often to the perplexity of children at school—more properly fall within the province of literary criticism. Inference and judgment are often considered part of reading, and there is indeed a skill in looking for the evidence. But fundamentally, reading novels rests on the same basic process as any other form of reading—asking questions and knowing how to find the answers in the print.

I should again point out that the questions we ask in reading are almost invariably implicit; we are not generally aware of the questions that we ask or even that we are asking them. But the fact that we are unaware of the questions does not mean that they are not being asked. They are like the questions that we ask in making sense of spoken language and of the world in general. We usually become aware of the need for such questions only when we lack them (and we are bewildered) or when they mislead us (and we are surprised).

Not only are we generally unaware of our questions as we read, we are also not often aware that we are getting answers, or of how we find these answers in the distinctive features of print. The answers in each case lie in the distinctive features of the print on the page. What we are unaware of is not the process of selecting and evaluating these answers, but the consequences of the process, the decisions made by the brain. We are aware of letters, or words, or general meaning, depending on what we are looking for.

These two closely related skills that we usually perform without awareness—asking appropriate questions and finding relevant answers—lie at the heart of reading. Yet these are not skills that are expressly taught. Indeed it is difficult to see how anyone could claim to teach such skills since there is very little that can be said specifically about either the nature of the questions or the source of the answers. But then, it is obviously not necessary that these skills should be taught specifically, since all of us have learned to read without the benefit of such instruction.

Other aspects of reading are also critical, such as achieving the right balance of visual and nonvisual information so that we are not afflicted by tunnel vision; not reading so slowly that short-term memory is overwhelmed; not trying to memorize so much that comprehension is affected; predicting; and learning to identify and understand unfamiliar words from context and from similarity to words already known. Readers even acquire a working knowledge of phonics, which means that rather than expecting to sound out unfamiliar words in isolation they learn to use spelling-to-sound correspondences to help select among a few possible alternatives. Very little of all these aspects of reading, you will notice, is expressly taught. How then does anyone ever learn to read?

Summary

There are many different kinds of text and many different purposes for reading. The one aspect of reading all have in common is that questions are asked of the text. Comprehension occurs when answers to these questions are found. Letter identification, word identification, and the comprehension of meaning are independent consequences of asking different kinds of questions of text. Comprehension need not require word identification, which in turn need not require letter identification.

The ability to ask relevant questions and to know where to find answers in text depends on familiarity with the type of material involved and the particular purpose of the reading. None of this can be taught explicitly, but it develops with the practice of reading.

7

Learning to Read

The phrase "learning to read" can be misleading, if it leads to an assumption that there is a magical day in every literate person's life, some kind of a threshold, on which we become a reader but before which we are merely learning to read. We begin learning to read the first time we make sense of print, and we learn something about reading every time we read.

On the other hand there is very little we can learn about reading without reading—and in this context I am referring specifically to reading written words in sequences and settings where they make sense. I am not referring to drills and exercises with letters, syllables, nonsense words, or even words when they are in sequences and situations where they have no purpose and make no sense. Children do not need nonsense in order to learn to read; they need to read.

The notion that learning to read is different from reading becomes particularly dangerous with older students having difficulty reading, who may be restricted to activities that do not make sense to them in order that they can "acquire basic skills." But the truly basic skills of reading, discussed throughout this book and summarized at the end of the preceding chapter, can never be taught directly and are only accessible to learners through the experience of reading. Not only does meaningful reading provide the essential clues and feedback for learning to read, it provides its own reinforcement. In less technical terms, learning to read is a *satisfying* activity. What encourages children to read and thus to learn to read is not some "extrinsic reward" like praise or high marks or a special treat, but being able to read. Watch children engrossed in a book from which they are learning about reading, and there will be no need to ask where the fundamental satisfaction lies.

The Roots of Reading

How do children begin reading in the first place? "Learning to read by reading" may seem to presuppose that there is already some reading ability as a basis for further learning. But how does reading get started?

There are two questions, one practical and the other theoretical. The theoretical question is "Where do the roots of reading lie; what are the basic insights that children need in order to begin to read?" The practical question is "How can children develop reading ability before they know sufficient words to read any book?" There is a simple answer to the practical question so I shall mention it briefly and then postpone the detailed discussion for a while. If children cannot read well enough to learn by reading, then someone else has to do their reading for them. The other question is far more basic and important, though it is asked less often: Where do the roots of reading lie? That is the question I want to deal with first.

Several fundamental insights are required before children can even begin to learn to read, although these first steps in reading are almost invariably overlooked in discussions of how reading should be "taught." For example, it is obvious that children must be able to distinguish written words from each other. They must learn that one arrangement of printed marks stands for the word (or rather the meaning) "horse" while another arrangement stands for "cow," and so forth. But learning to recognize individual words is something that goes on through life, at least fifty thousand times for a moderately competent reader as I have pointed out. Underlying this very general ability is a fundamental insight that each reader must have once, but only once. This insight is that the visible marks that are written language are meaningful, that there is some point in distinguishing them at all. Print is not arbitrary like the pattern of the wallpaper or the decoration around the label on a jar; different patterns of print must be treated differently. The differences are significant.

No one ever teaches a child all this. We take it for granted when we tell children that a certain squiggle "says" their name, or that another is the word "dog," that they know what we are talking about and have intuited that print has a complex meaningful function. We leave children to achieve their own understanding of this. But until the realization clicks that printed marks are distinguishable from each other in ways that make a difference in the world, that they have a *use*, reading cannot begin. I am not sure how children first get this essential insight but I can give an example of a child who had just achieved it.

The child was Matthew, barely three years old and certainly not a reader by most criteria. He could recognize only a few words (his name and one or two words in favorite picture books) and had not yet mastered all the letters of the alphabet. But in a department store he knew how people located the section that sold greeting cards. He pointed to a sign hanging over the greeting card counter and correctly explained "that sign says 'cards.'" How did he know? It would not be particularly interesting if Matthew had been able to identify the word because his parents had "taught" it to him; that would not demonstrate that he understood the function of words. He might merely have learned to parrot a response to a particular printed mark, just as he might have learned quite meaninglessly to call a certain object a "dictionary" without having any understanding of what a dictionary was. But in another department Matthew was confronted by a word that was certainly unfamiliar. He took one look at the word *luggage*, glanced around him, and said that the word must be "cases." Here in this "error" was the clue that Matthew had the insight that print has meaning. He was able to impose a meaning on a word—to *predict* a meaning for it—when indeed he was not able to recognize that particular word.

What other insights are there? One must be that the printed marks that are words can be broken down into smaller units called letters that have some relation to spoken language—a necessary prerequisite for phonics. Many children find this an extremely difficult insight to achieve, presumably because individual letters do not "make sense" in the way that a whole word can be meaningful. Who can point to an "A" or an "L" or a "W" as something meaningful in the world around us? One six-year-old who knew quite a lot about reading complained as she struggled with the printed word *dog* under a picture of a dog: "I know this word is 'dog' and I could read it even if the picture wasn't there, but I don't understand what I'm supposed to do with this 'dee' and 'oh' and 'gee' the teacher keeps talking about."

Every reader needs the insight that the printed words in a book are *language*, that they can be interpreted in terms of a story or useful information. We hear a lot about the importance of a literate home, of growing up in an environment of books, but what exactly does a child learn from such surroundings? Reading is not "caught" from exposure to books, like an infection. What sense does a child make out of them? It is not an explanation to say that a child hears an adult reading a story and therefore understands that the adult is getting the words from the text. Many adults understand that music comes from the loudspeakers of a record player without understanding exactly how the sounds are related to the groove on the record. How is a child to know that putting a book into the hands of an adult does not generate or inspire the sounds of reading aloud in the same way that putting a record on a record player seems magically to make music come out of a recording?

Of course, from our superior position of knowing how to read we think it ludicrous—if we think about it at all—that reading might be a complete mystery to a child, something more akin to a ritual than a skill. But we are looking at the situation from a very favored position. Like many experts, we tend to underrate the intelligence of the outsider who cannot see at once what is so obvious to us.

Understanding that printed marks have differences that are significant, that written words can be associated with meaning in some way, and that there are relationships between print and spoken language—all these are insights that a beginning reader must acquire. They are not immediately obvious yet they stand at the threshold of reading. As is so often the case, the things we take most for granted are those in greatest need of explanation.

What teachers are more likely to call "readiness" for reading seems to me to be of less significance. For example, research has shown that many children have difficulty understanding special terms like "word," "letter," "sentence," and so forth, not to mention in discriminating all the different sounds that their spoken language is supposed to consist of. But the concepts of "letter," "word," and "sentence" are difficult for prereaders for the simple reason that they are not part of spoken language. They seem obvious to readers *because* they can read. Certainly there is nothing like a "letter" in spoken language. When we comprehend spoken language we do not break it down into sounds like "duh-oh-guh is 'dog,' " the way we sometimes talk about speech in reading instruction. We do not separate the elements of speech—into—units—like—this. A word is something that exists in *written* language; something with a white space on either side. And who ever talks about a "sentence" in normal speech? The only person who would say "Did you hear my sentence just now?" rather than "Did you hear what I just said?" is a judge. As far as I can see, knowledge of the meaning of these specialized terms has nothing to do with reading. Many children learn to read, even teach themselves to read, without understanding what these words mean, just as they learn to talk before comprehending (if ever) such grammatical terms as noun, verb, adjective, and so forth. If knowledge of specialized terms has any relevance in learning to read, it is in making sense of the instruction that is given. If a teacher makes it important for children to know the meaning of words like "letter," "word," "syllable," and "paragraph," or if a teacher expects children to demonstrate the very complicated and artificial skill of detecting separate and meaningful "sounds" in spoken language, then obviously children who cannot do these things will have difficulty in learning to read. But difficulty in following particular kinds of instruction should not mean that a child is not ready to learn to read; it simply underlines that instruction can be inappropriate and even confusing.

Making Sense of Learning to Read

Clearly, reading has many facets that must be mastered in a variety of different situations. Nevertheless, I think there is one general answer to the question of how children learn to read, and that is *by making sense of written language*. A corollary to this statement is that children do not learn to read from nonsense.

Childen do not learn to read in order to make sense of print. They strive to make sense of print and as a consequence learn to read. This order of events is identical with the way in which spoken language is learned. Children do not learn to talk in order to "communicate" and to make sense of the language that they hear. As they try to make sense of the language they hear spoken around them, they learn to understand speech and to employ it themselves. There is nothing remarkable about this phenomenon; in fact, understanding that children's first efforts are always to make sense of the world removes much of the mystery from how they come to master spoken and written language. Children would never learn to talk if they waited for us to teach them speech the way we often try to teach them to read, one meaningless bit after another. But children strive to make sense of the environment they are in, provided the environment has the possibility of making sense in the first place. Children can make sense of spoken and written language in the way that they make sense of everything else in their world. They are only confounded by nonsense.

We tend to forget that the majority of children grow up in a world in which they are surrounded by print, almost all of it meaningful, just as they develop spoken language in environments where they are immersed in meaningful spoken language. It is a mistake to equate the written language environment of children with the number of books they see in their homes. Children do not *need* the supposed advantage of "literate" parents—unless it is falsely assumed that children who do not come from "literate" backgrounds will somehow be incapable of learning to read.

Try to look at the world through a child's eyes. As you walk through a supermarket you are bombarded by print from all sides and from above—product labels, packages, prices, posters, slogans, lists, directions, greeting cards, magazines, wrappers—much of which repeats print found in the home or eventually finds its way there. As adults we tend to pay little conscious attention to all this print, for the simple reason that it is so familiar to us. We take it for granted. But to a child the print is a constant challenge, a persistent problem, something that must and can be made sense of.

Few children are completely unaware of telephone directories and catalogs, of magazines and newspapers with their sports pages, entertainment guides, and comic strips. Out in the street there are traffic signs, store fronts, advertising, menus, mailboxes, posters, billboards, and doors labeled with very significant print. Practically every piece of equipment in town and country bears a manufacturer's name and some significant words like *fuel level*, *lights*, or *on* and *off*. And just about all of this ocean of print is meaningful, it makes a difference. When the word STOP occurs in the real world it is not a pointless series of squiggles with no relation to anything else around. It is not there for people to read aloud, to decode into spoken language, to bark "st-o-puh, stop" at each other. The written word STOP means "Here's where you have to stop." It makes sense. It can be used.

Think of the print on television; not only the representations of people reading in so many aspects of daily life, but the written language that is part of every commercial. The text of television commercials is among the most informative written language that children can see, since at the same time that words are presented visually—the product name and perhaps some words like *new! improved!*—the same words are often spoken aloud and accompanied by a picture that demonstrates the meaning of the message.

A child is surrounded by written language and learns to read by making sense of it, solving problems like, Why is it there? Why do people respond to different examples of it in different ways? What does it signify? Children must discover the different ways in which various examples of print have to be interpreted, and remember how to distinguish one form from another in the future. But these problems are no different in essence from the cat and dog problem, learning how to distinguish one thing from another, which children of preschool age solve with ease thousands of times. Written language presents problems but in the real world it also contains the clues to their solution. Every meaningful bit of print not only helps children to gain the general insights they need about the nature and functions of written language, but also offers specific hints about the likely meanings of particular words. Because print in the real world is so often meaningful it also provides the test for the solutions that children hypothesize. Children quickly discover if they have correctly read the words *closed*, *no exit*, *cards*, *gum*, or *women*.

Not that adults have nothing to do with all this learning. There is an extremely critical role that adults play in helping children in this fundamental task of making sense of print, and that is to make sense of print for them. Just as adults almost unwittingly make it possible for children to learn spoken language by talking to them in situations that make sense, so adults can help children master print by the simple practice of reading to them the print to which their attention is drawn. All of the specific specialized aspects of reading—like using telephone directories, consulting menus, checking catalogs—are learned through guidance and models contributed by people who know how to do these things. It is not so much a matter of teaching these skills to children as doing them alongside children, showing how the skill is performed.

When children need to know something about print—or when their attention can be drawn to print—on a package, on a street sign, in an advertisement—there is an opportunity for an adult to help them to learn to read by doing the reading for them. Anything in the world of print surrounding children can be read to them with profit. Telling children what a written word says will not solve their problems for them, any more than calling an animal by its name solves the cat and dog problem, but the assistance provides children with the opportunity to solve problems for themselves. And they will solve the problem of distinguishing words in the same way that they solve the problem of distinguishing dogs and cats—by looking for and testing hypotheses about significant differences.

Of course, it does not hurt for a child to have some aquaintance with the alphabet. For an adult to say "See how these two words both begin with *B*" might be helpful in drawing a child's attention to distinctive aspects of print. But learning the alphabet is not a prerequisite for learning to distinguish words, and the alphabet can be a handicap if adults use it to try and train children to sound out words before they are able to make sense of what the adults are talking about. Being able to recognize words makes sense of learning letters.

It is an excellent idea for children to have stories read to them, but initially at least, the isolated but meaningful words and fragments of sentences that children naturally meet in the world of print around them are probably as important in getting them started in reading as formal sessions around a book. Reading stories to children has two general advantages, however. The first is the insight that interesting stories are associated with the printed marks in books can have a highly motivating effect on children—provided of course that the stories are genuinely interesting and are not forced upon a child. The second advantage of reading to children is that it acquaints them with the peculiarities and conventions of written language, which is not the same as speech. Written and spoken language may employ the same vocabulary and roughly the same grammar, but the style of written language tends to be more formal, less personal, and more abstract. Children need to become acquainted with the language of books; it is not the language they hear spoken around them in their daily life, and it is unrealistic to expect them to learn this unfamiliar style at the same time that they learn to read.

One distinctive aspect of the written language of stories is that its meaning is usually completely removed from any kind of external support or verification. If children do not understand what somebody says to them in the home or street, they can usually get clues to the meaning from the general situation, and even from facial expressions and other gestures. But doubt about written language has to be resolved from the text itself (except sometimes for limited clues provided by illustrations) and experience is required to develop the habit of using the thread of an argument or story as a clue to the meaning of language. Children can acquire this experience by having written language read to them.

There is no need for concern that children who have the words on candy wrappers or the text of schoolbooks read to them will become lazy and reluctant to read for themselves. Children allow adults or other children to read for them for just as long and as much as they are unable to read themselves. As they develop competence in reading they will take over from a person reading for them. Their impatience soon shows when they are forced to listen to something they can read for themselves.

Joining the Literacy Club

Many children can read before they come to school, so obviously formal instruction is not essential. And they are by no means just the most privileged of children. Many come from large families, single parent homes, poor neighborhoods, and are not especially favored academically. If they arrived at school unable to read it would be predicted that they would have great difficulty doing so. Yet already they can read. What enabled them to get the necessary understanding?

Whether children have become readers before arriving at school or not, they obviously require particular conditions if they are to achieve the insights and develop the skills of literacy. The meaningfulness of written language does not make itself immediately apparent to anyone. I have discussed how adept children are at learning, if print is meaningful to them. The question remains concerning the exact nature of the circumstances in which this learning ability is manifested—and of the circumstances when it is not. Where are the roots of literacy planted? How must they be nurtured? To understand reading children must become members of a group of written language users, they must *join the literacy club.*

Children can join the literacy club with a single unqualified reciprocal act of affiliation. There are no dues to be paid, no entry standards to be met. A mutual acknowledgment of acceptance into a group of people who use written language is all that is required. Children who join the literacy club take it for granted that they will become like the more experienced members of the club; they are the same kind of people. The experienced members of the club take it for granted that the children will be like them; they are the same kind of people. Expectation does not guarantee learning, of course, but it makes it possible. Expectation that learning will *not* take place almost inevitably produces that effect.

There is nothing special about the literacy club. It functions in much the same way as any other special interest group. Members are concerned about each other's interests and welfare. But in particular, members occupy themselves with whatever activities the club has formed itself to promote, constantly demonstrating the value and utility of these activities to the new members, helping them to participate in these activities themselves when they want, but never forcing their involvement. And never discriminating against them for lacking the understanding or expertise of more practiced members. Differences in ability and in specific interests are taken for granted.

Here are some advantages of membership in the written language club for children:

- They see what written language does. The uses of written language are complex and manifold; written language can probably be employed in support of every human endeavor. The multiplicity of ways in which written language makes sense in our world is demonstrated to children by the "people like them" who already belong to the club.
- Children are admitted as junior members. No one expects them to read or to write like more experienced members of the club, but no one doubts that they will do so in due course. They are not labeled. Errors are expected, not frowned upon or punished as undesirable behavior.

- Members help newcomers to become experts. There is no formal instruction, no special time when they are expected to learn. Instead, someone helps children to read what they are trying to read and to write what they might try to write. The child is told what the sign says, is shown where the label indicates the contents, is assisted in preparing the shopping list or writing the birthday greeting. The help is always relevant, so that children are never confused about what it is for. Formal instruction may indeed on occasion be asked for or offered, but always it is relevant to something the child is trying to do, and always it is under the control of the child.
- Children are quickly admitted into a full range of club activities, as they make sense to them and are useful to them. They are never required to be involved in something they do not understand or that appears to be pointless. Everything that reading and writing can do for other members of the club is revealed to them, in the expectation that they in turn will make use of reading and writing in the same way. They always have opportunities to test their hypotheses, to find out what written language will do for them, and how to do these things.
- Perhaps most importantly, children learn to identify themselves as members of the literacy club. They see themselves as readers and as writers. We learn and behave like the people we see ourselves as being. If we belong to a club, then everything pertaining to the club comes to us naturally, as of right. But if we are excluded from the club, or if we exclude ourselves, then we deliberately constrain ourselves from acting like members of the club. We learn not to be like members of the club. Such constraints are all the more potent because they are unconscious; we do not recognize that we are holding ourselves back.
- All of the learning takes place without risk. There are no formal tests, no examinations, and no one expects new members to be as good as each other or to "progress" at the same rate. There are no planned schedules of learning, no curriculum committees, no accountability, no objectives, no prerequisites, and nothing is tested except in use.

Recent research in a number of cultures has shown that many children know much about reading and writing before they get to school, or independently of what they are taught in school. They know many of the uses of written language, its role in signs, labels, lists, letters, books, magazines, catalogs, computer programs, and television guides. They know what people do with written language, even if they cannot do these things themselves. They also have rough ideas about how written language works, that it consists of letters written on lines, that it is laid out in conventional ways, and that there are rules and regularities of spelling. They pretend to read and to write in their role-playing games.

Why should children join such a club, even before they know a thing about reading and writing themselves? Because they see people around them engaging in meaningful written language activities, and because they see themselves as being like those people and are accepted in such a way.

There is nothing unusual in any of this. It is precisely the way infants learn to talk and to understand spoken language. No one gives babies formal instruction and examinations in how adults use spoken language; few would learn to talk if they did. Instead, infants almost from the moment of birth are admitted into a club of spoken language users, of "people like them," who speak in the way the babies in due course are expected to speak. In due course the babies do speak in that way.

There are some unique advantages in joining the literacy club. With spoken language you need to do your learning from people who are already in the club, who are usually in range of your sight as well as your hearing. In the literacy club you can learn from members who are far distant, who may even no longer be living. In the literacy club you can learn from *authors*.

Margaret Spencer has argued that it is the authors of children's stories who most fully teach children how to read. The children follow a familiar or predictable tale, perhaps with another reader's assistance, and the author shows how the story is actually told in written language. It is tragic, she says, that in the name of "reading instruction" teachers often come between children and authors.

Reading and Writing

Because this book is specifically concerned with an analysis of reading, I have had very little to say about writing most of the time. But in the current chapter, when the concern has been with learning to read, reference to writing has been unavoidable. Reading and writing can no more be dealt with separately in learning than they should be in teaching.

I do not even refer to children joining the reading club (or the writing club), but only to the literacy club, or the club of written language users. Children learn about both reading and writing in learning the uses of written language. The distinguishable "skills" of reading and writing are relatively superficial aspects of literacy. The insights and understanding that I have been emphasizing about the meaningfulness of written language and its manifold utility are basic to both reading and writing. Everything a child learns about reading helps in becoming a writer. Everything learned about writing contributes to reading ability. To keep the two activities separate does more than deprive them of their basic sense, it impoverishes any learning that might take place.

Summary

To learn to read children must see ways of employing reading to further their own aims and interests. If written language is made meaningful to them, they will learn in exactly the same way that they learn about spoken language. Children need others to read to them, and for them, until they can read for themselves. Stories are important and helpful—especially because children learn a great deal about reading from authors—but so also are signs, labels, and the other working print in the environment. Children must be fully accepted into the literacy club, so that they can receive all the different kinds of demonstration and collaboration they require to become readers themselves.

8

The Teacher's Role

I have tried to show that children "know" implicitly how to solve the problems of learning to read. And indeed, children must be trusted to know how to learn since the most important aspects of reading cannot be taught. What then is the role of the teacher? What is the point of "teaching reading" in school?

What takes place in the classroom is critical for many children, since it can determine whether they become readers or not. A teacher is one of the most important people in the beginning reader's life, in establishing the child in the literacy club, and can make the difference between success and failure. Schools may not be held wholly responsible for the degree to which children succeed in becoming literate. Nevertheless, teachers have a crucial part to play.

HELPING VERSUS INTERFERING

Simply stated, teachers must facilitate and promote the admission of every child into the literacy club. Children who come to school already members of the club, who regard themselves as the kind of people who read and write, should find expanded opportunities in school for engaging in all the activities of club membership. Children who have not become members before they arrive in school should find the classroom the place where they are immediately inducted into the club. The classroom should be a place for meaningful and useful reading (and writing) activities, where participation is possible without evaluation or compulsion, and collaboration is always available. No child should be excluded.

Children have to make sense of reading so teachers must make sure that reading—and learning to read—makes sense to children. Children learn to read by reading, so teachers must help children to read by making reading easy, not by making it difficult. These remarks may sound obvious, except for the fact that a good deal that is done at school—and also sometimes by well-meaning adults out of school—has the consequence of making learning to read more difficult. Since a major concern of a teacher must always be not to get in the way of children's learning to read, I shall begin my specific remarks about the role of teachers with a list of negatives. I have termed the items on this list "Easy Ways to Make Learning to Read Difficult," because all too often they are urged upon teachers as rules that are supposed to help children to read.

Interfering with Learning to Read

Nine rules of reading instruction that teachers would do well *not* to follow are:

1. *Aim for early mastery of the rules of reading.* There are no rules of reading, at least none that can be specified with sufficient precision to make a child a reader. The implicit knowledge of how to read that experienced readers have acquired has been developed through reading, and not through exercises or drills. Only reading provides the necessary practice in identifying words on sight (not figuring them out letter by letter); in using prior knowledge and context to identify words and meanings with a minimum of visual information (not struggling blindly and pointlessly to identify one word after another); in predicting, looking for meaning, reading fast rather than slowly, confidently rather than cautiously; in using short-term memory efficiently so that it is not overloaded and even the most meaningful of texts made nonsense. Most of the drills that children are given to help them to read become useful—and easy—only after skill in reading has been developed. Better readers are always more efficient at knowing the alphabet, knowing the "sounds of letters," and blending letter sounds together to make words, because these are all tasks that become deceptively simple with experience in reading. But they are difficult if not impossible before children understand what reading is.
2. *Ensure that phonic skills are learned and used.* Children do not need a mastery of phonics in order to identify words that they have not met in print before. The very complexity and unreliability of the 166 rules and scores of exceptions make it remarkable that anyone should think that inability to use phonics explains "Why Johnny still can't read." Once a child discovers what a word is in a meaningful context, learning to recognize it on another occasion is as simple as learning to recognize a face on a second occasion, and does not

need phonics. Discovering what a word is in the first place is usually most efficiently accomplished by asking someone, listening to someone else read the word, or using context to provide a substantial clue.

3. *Teach letters or words one at a time, making sure each one is learned before moving on.* Another widespread misconception is that children have difficulty remembering the names of objects and words and letters, and that only constant repetition will help fix a name in a child's mind. For a dozen years from about the age of two or three children learn at least a thousand new words a year, often after hearing a word used only once or twice. It has been calculated that eight-year-old children must learn nearly thirty new words daily. Children do not get the credit for such fantastic feats of learning because the learning takes place so effortlessly and inconspicuously.

   Children do not learn all these words by rote—by studying lists of a dozen new words at a time or by doing exercises given to them by adults. By criticizing phonics I am not recommending a "whole word" approach. Children learn by making sense of words that are meaningful to them in context; they learn through comprehension. We have not become fluent readers by learning how to recognize fifty thousand or more written words on sight; we have learned to recognize all these words in the process of becoming fluent readers, in the act of meaningful reading.

4. *Make word-perfect reading a prime objective.* Because of the limit on the amount of new visual information from the eyes that the brain can handle, and the limit on how much can be retained in short-term memory, emphasis on visual information makes reading difficult. To read efficiently—and also to learn to read—it is necessary to make maximum use of what is already known. It usually does not matter if readers fail to get a word or two exactly right—provided they are reading sense—because context will make it clear if an error that makes a difference has been made. On the other hand, overconcern with accuracy directs too much attention to individual words, in effect treating them as if they were out of context, with the result that the visual system is overwhelmed. Most children seem to know intuitively that reading is a matter of getting meaning correct rather than identifying particular words, no doubt because the strain of focusing undue attention on individual words makes reading a difficult and nonsensical activity.

5. *Discourage guessing; insist that children read carefully.* I have stressed the importance of prediction in comprehension and in the

identification of unfamiliar words. Efficient readers make maximum use of a minimum of visual information because taking too many pains to avoid making mistakes will have the paradoxical effect of interfering with comprehension and accuracy.

Even in learning to read—in fact, especially in learning to read—slowness has only one consequence, it adds to the burden on short-term memory, making comprehension less likely and thus making reading more difficult. For children as for fluent readers, the only practical solution at times of difficulty is to speed up, to read on, and to try to find the general sense that will make it possible to go back, if necessary, to identify or comprehend specific words.

6. *Insist upon word-perfect reading.* No one can learn names correctly, whether of dogs and cats, letters or words, unless there is a possibility of being wrong. The "experimental" hypothesis-testing basis of learning necessitates taking chances. Children learn naturally not by rote memorization or by reckless guessing but by trying to assess whether something might be the case. Adults who treat reading errors as stupidities, jokes, or transgressions—or who encourage other children to do the same—do more than misperceive the basic nature of reading, they also block a principle way in which reading is learned. Many of the apparent mistakes that children make in reading aloud are not errors of sense, but rather a matter of being unable to do an additional task at the same time as reading meaningfully, namely speaking in a language that is unfamiliar. It is not uncommon for any reader—beginner or experienced—to read aloud a sentence like *Back she came* as "She came back," or *He has no money* as "He hasn't any money" or even "He ain't got no money." The reader is getting the meaning of the text well enough but is putting it into a familiar language, the way the reader would normally talk. It is unreasonable to expect children not only to understand text but to speak aloud in a particular language style that may seem forced, artificial, and even nonsensical to them.

7. *Correct errors immediately.* A certain way to make children anxious, hesitant, and otherwise inefficient readers is to jump on errors the moment they occur. This discouraging habit is sometimes justified as "providing immediate feedback," but in fact it may not be relevant to what the child is trying to do, and may in the long run discourage children from relying on their own judgment for self-correction when they have made a mistake.

Not only can correction come too soon, it can be misguided. A child reading aloud in class who pauses before a word is frequently supplied with that word instantly, by other children if not by the teacher. But the pause may not reflect doubt about that particular word. The child may already have made a tentative silent identification and be wondering what that word has to do with words that have already been read or even with what the child has seen coming up a few words ahead. Once again a word-for-word emphasis can have the result of persuading a learner that reading is an activity in which sense plays little part.

8. *Identify and treat problem readers as early as possible.* There are many reasons why children may seem to make slow progress at the beginning of learning to read. They may not yet understand what reading is about, they may not be interested in learning to read, they may be apprehensive about the teacher or other adults who want them to learn to read, they may resent the whole idea of school. They may not understand the language in which their schoolbooks are written, or the language that their teacher uses to talk about reading. They may even have started off on the wrong foot— possibly because they have learned too well, for example by assimilating the notion that if they learn how to decode and identify individual words they will be able to read and sense will take care of itself.

There are two reasons why identifying such children as problem readers or as "handicapped" or learning disabled in some way is not a good way to help them. The first reason is that children so labeled immediately become anxious and expect not to perform as well as other children, and their general perception of their own abilities suffers. They exclude themselves from the literacy club. In the short run, even for competent readers, such attitudes are completely disabling. Create anxiety in a competent reader (for example by providing difficult material) and reading can be made almost impossible. The reader begins to strive for accuracy, pays far too much attention to every word, and is practically blinded by tunnel vision and the overload on short-term memory. To label children as problem readers early in their lives may create a problem where there was no need for one originally.

The second reason why the label of "poor reader" can be so disabling to children—all the way through their school careers—is that very often the "solution" for such a problem is more of the same treatment that caused it in the first place. They find themselves excluded from the literacy club even if they want to belong. Children identified as poor readers are often deprived of opportunities to read, put onto the much harder task of trying to sound out isolated words or words in meaningless sequences. Students who have had reading problems for ten years do not need more of the conditions that have contributed to their failure.

9. *Use every opportunity during reading instruction to improve spelling and written expression, and also insist on the best possible spoken English.* Being able to spell has nothing to do with reading. We can all read words that we cannot spell, and being able to spell a word does little to help us read it. I am not saying that other language skills are not important, but that they can complicate a reading task. If the aim at one particular time is to help a child become fluent in reading, expecting the child also to worry about answering questions, writing answers, and avoiding errors of spelling and of grammar is simply to overload the reading task and to make learning to read more difficult.

Similarly, spoken English is largely irrelevant to reading. Children forced to worry about their pronunciation as they read aloud will not become better readers. Expecting children to read in what to them may be a completely unnatural style contributes to giving a totally false idea of what reading is.

Helping Children Learn to Read

Two questions perhaps arise. The first might be that it is all very well for me to provide a set of negative statements about what teachers should endeavor to avoid, but what should a teacher *do*? If there is little sense in a lot of drill and exercise, what instead should be going on in the reading classroom? The second question might be that my list of cautions about interfering with children learning to read implies that the children are already capable of some reading in the first place. What does a teacher do about a child who cannot read at all? How does a teacher get the child started in the literacy club? The answers to both questions are the same, since there is basically only one problem: how to facilitate reading for children when they can read very little or not at all. The answers can be summed up in one basic rule and guideline for every aspect of reading instruction—*make learning to read easy*—which means making reading a meaningful, enjoyable, useful, and *frequent* experience for children.

Put in another way, the solution requires that the teacher should ensure there is someone, if only another child, to *read for children what they cannot read for themselves.* If a child cannot read at all, the teacher or other helpful reader must do all the reading (or provide the necessary clues) for the child.

Reading on behalf of children helps them to achieve three important objectives in beginning to read and continuing to learn to read:

1. *Understanding the functions of print.* It is in being read to, or read for, that children find the opportunity to gain the insight that print has purposes. Children cannot be *told* that written language is a varied part of the environment that can be as meaningful, useful, and satisfying as speech. Children must experience that insight for themselves; they must be put into situations where the insight can develop.

2. *Gaining familiarity with written language.* Spoken and written language are put together in distinctive ways. The particular conventions of written language can make it quite unpredictable, and therefore difficult to comprehend. Constructions that are common in children's books, such as *What splendid teeth the beaver has,* or *Down the road hand in hand ran Susie and her friend* seem simple and straightforward to most of us only because of our familiarity with written language; they are not the kind of language anyone is likely to be accustomed to from everyday speech. The only way children can become familiar with written language, before they can extend their knowledge by reading for themselves, is by being read to.

3. *Getting the chance to learn.* It is important to read to children, but even more important to read *with* them. Children get their first chance to solve many of the problems of reading when they and adults are reading the same text at the same time. It does not matter that at the beginning the children may recognize none of the words they are looking at, indeed it is in the process of being confronted by words that are unknown that they find the motivation and opportunity to begin to distinguish and recognize particular words, in the same way that the cat and dog problem is solved. Children reading along with an adult or other reader will look out for the words that they know, and they will select for themselves the additional words that they want to learn or practice.

An interesting change takes place as an adult and child read together. Initially the child's eyes wander over the pages and then follow along behind as the child strives to grasp some understanding of the relationship between the marks on the page and what is being said. But as the child develops a little proficiency in reading—especially if the passage being read is from a poem or story well-known to the child—then the child's eyes move ahead of the reader's voice. The child begins reading independently of the adult assistance. The situation is not unlike learning to ride a bicycle. For as long as the child needs adult help then the child cycles slower than the adult pushes. But as competence and confidence develop, so the child tends to pull ahead of the adult until eventually able to manage alone. No need to fear that a child who is helped at the beginning will become lazy or overly dependent on adults. The child who can take over from the adult in reading will be no more content to lag behind than the child riding the bicycle. Mastery provides its own incentive; children who can manage their own buttons and shoelaces rarely tolerate adults who insist on doing these tasks for them.

Making Sense of All Kinds of Print

In stressing the importance of reading to children I do not want to give the impression that I am talking just about *books*. In fact, I think that the widespread emphasis on books in school constitutes a distorted and often obstructive approach to reading instruction. Indeed, the only books that should be read to children or that they should be required to read for themselves are the ones that genuinely interest them, that contain fascinating rhymes and stories rather than the bland and unnatural prose to which many children are expected to attend, whether recounting a boring day in the life of an insipid pair of fictitious children or relating that *Sam can fan the fat cat*. The print that offers beginning readers the most insights into the meaningfulness of written language tends to lie outside books in the far more personal and pervasive world of their own lives. Children may learn more of the basics of reading from the brand name above a garage, the words on a candy wrapper, or the experience of their own name on a pair of boots, than from any number of books and exercises. In natural, out-of-school surroundings, printed words exist not to be associated with *sounds* but with *sense*. Chalked on a board in the classroom or printed below a picture in a book, the letters T-O-Y-S have no function, no point. But when the same marks occur in a store they convey the distinct and important meaning "This is where the toys can be bought."

The wealth of meaningful print in the environment of children can be read to them, not in any obtrusive or demanding manner but as casually and naturally as the objects in a child's environment are named. Just as children are told "There's a big dog" or "See the plane?" so adults can say "That says 'ketchup' " and "There's the 'One-Way' sign." This simple practice will give children the opportunity to derive insights, generate ideas, and test hypotheses about reading while they retain the freedom to select and control what they most want to learn whenever it makes the most sense to them. In such circumstances children learn about print and about reading in the same way that they learn about spoken language, without obvious effort or the need for formal instruction.

Reading in School

Total immersion in meaningful print is hardly a typical experience for most children in school, nor indeed can all the conditions that facilitate learning to read be easily translated into the classroom. It is difficult for teachers to duplicate the richness of print that occurs naturally in the outside world, an example of the many differences between school and the world at large that children can find so confusing.

Nevertheless, there are many ways in which children in school can experience printed language that has both interest and a meaning for them. Teachers can try to ensure that children often have the opportunity to read—or to hear—stories that have an intrinsic appeal, to which they will voluntarily give attention. Teachers can also make frequent use of print to forward a significant activity in some way, whether in play (keeping a store, publishing a newspaper) or in the daily routine. Printed materials and products that make sense to children in the outside world can be brought into the classroom. And there are a number of ways in which print can be emphasized in the functions of the school, for example in the identification of various classrooms and offices, washrooms and storage rooms, lockers and coathooks (all of which are often labeled too high for young children's eyes.) Menus—both the restaurant and the computer variety—constitute meaningful print, and so do posters, notices, direction signs, maps, catalogs, timetables, and telephone books, especially if they can be produced in a format children can handle, a print they can discriminate easily, and a language they can understand. Not only can these and other familiar materials be used to help children learn more about reading, but they also offer the only opportunity many children may have of learning to use or make sense of the materials themselves. And, of course, much of it can be produced by the children. No one ever learned to use a telephone directory from a lecture; it is specific practice at a specific task, with sympathetic help in meaningful situations, that makes the learning of any skill possible.

At the same time that a wealth of meaningful print is provided, much of the print that is meaningless could be removed from the scene.

There may be occasional justification for the use of individual letters and even isolated words as part of the decor, and lists of useful words (like the days of the week or months of the year) can at times have value for reference purposes. But in general the tendency should be resisted to decorate walls with sheets of print whose only function is perhaps to give adults the impression of an educational atmosphere. There is usually little need for a frenzy of labeling at the expense of windows, pictures, and even soothing sections of blank wall.

Of course, providing a print-rich environment and endeavoring to avoid interference with the natural ability of children to learn does not constitute a "program" for reading instruction. I cannot provide a consumers' report on all the different reading methodologies. The only conclusion to draw from the analysis I have made is that no one can rely on a program to teach reading, in the form of a package that can be taken off a shelf or ordered from a publisher. Reading is not taught by prescription. There are hundreds of reading programs, many of which have little relevance to reading. But even the most sensible of programs will be little more than an aid to keeping children occupied while they are learning to read. Reading cannot be taught in the way that arithmetic is taught (not always successfully either), as a series of operations that children must learn sequentially and that can be ticked off and taken for granted as children show proficiency in each one. "Programmed instruction" scarcely scratches the surface of reading.

Teachers must make their own decisions about what needs to be done. The question should not be "Which method should I use?" but "How do I decide what to do now?" I have not argued that there should be no phonics, only that phonics has a widely unsuspected complexity and that children should be expected to learn about phonics only to the extent that they can make sense of the instruction. I have not said that children should not be taught the alphabet (it helps teachers and children communicate on the subject of written language), but until children have a good idea of what reading is, learning the names of letters is largely a nonsensical activity. The issue is always what a child can make sense of, and that changes with each individual teacher. Programs should not be expected to make decisions for teachers. The question is not a simple one of whether phonics, sight words, or language experience is the best approach.

I certainly do not argue that teachers should not know about the tools of their trade, about the multitude of programs, materials, and "activities" that are available for their use, although a listing and evaluation of all these items would be out of place in this book. Most of the training teachers receive on the subject of reading is devoted to lectures and demonstrations about different programs and methods. What is usually lacking is any kind of understanding of the nature of reading so that teachers can make up their own minds about when and how to use particular methods. Teachers often do not know what programs can reasonably be expected to be accomplished—how much for example a child can actually learn from phonic drills, or from sound-blending exercises—nor do they know the *cost* of such programs to the child in terms of memory overload, tunnel vision, rote learning, or boredom and confusion. Teachers must be discriminating, and that requires both a familiarity with programs and an understanding of reading. They must be able to see what makes sense.

Where teachers cannot save children from engaging in pointless activities and undergoing ritualistic tests, they can at least explain to children the difference. Children understand that they might be asked to do something just to keep them quiet, or because some authority arbitrarily wants it. The tragedy is when children are led to believe that nonsensical activities *are* reading.

The importance of formal programs and of kits of materials in reading instruction is grossly overrated. Many children have learned to read without special programs or materials at all, and many other children have probably learned despite their formal instruction. Everything I have said about reading in this book is contrary to approaches that demand sequenced instruction and constant measurement, and is therefore contrary to instruction teachers may themselves receive in their own training.

Problems of Programmatic Instruction

I have been critical of programs a number of times in this book and even more forcefully elsewhere. It is time perhaps for me to explain exactly what I am referring to by the term "programs," why they tend to be misguided if not totally wrong, and why nevertheless they are so pervasive in education and might become even more so.

By programs, or programmatic instruction, I refer to any endeavor by anyone outside the classroom to determine systematically and in advance what teachers and learners should do next in the classroom. Programmatic instruction typically involves predetermined activities, drills, exercises, prerequisites, questions and responses, right and wrong answers, scores, marks, grades, tests (many tests), objectives, entry behaviors, expected behaviors, criterion levels, and "accountability." Such instruction rarely engages children in meaningful reading enterprises (except in the mind of the program developer). The written language that is demonstrated, and to which children are expected to attend, tends to be fragmented, decontextualized, and trivial. If anything, such aspects of programs teach that written language is nonsensical and that no worthwhile club exists. Many program developers entertain the awesome belief that reading can be taught to a child one predetermined bit at a time.

All of this is the antithesis of admitting a child to the literacy club. None of the drills, exercises, and tests of formal programmatic instruction demonstrate that written language is meaningful or useful; their only purposes are their own instructional ends. The only evident reason for the child to attend to the task is to get it over with, to get the mark, or because the teacher says so.

Why then is so much reading instruction programmatic? Why do school systems buy programs (which is the sole reason publishers produce them)? One reason is that schools are strange institutions— one might almost argue that they are designed to prevent the formation of clubs. They are walled off from the meaningful world outside, with the children segregated into groups ideally so homogenized in age and ability that they will be unable to help each other, under the supervision of an isolated teacher with little time to engage personally in any worthwhile literate activities that the child can observe. Some teachers feel they need programmatic activities just to keep the lid on, to escape chaos.

A second reason for the pervasiveness of programs in education is inertia. Systematized instruction has been around for so long that many people cannot imagine education without it (just as many teachers cannot imagine learning taking place without constant tests and other forms of evaluation, although these are not characteristics of how children learn spoken language and other things out of school). Schools of education train new teachers to be dependent upon programs, sometimes because the professors know no better, sometimes because they can say it is what schools want or because it is what schools are like.

A third reason for programmatic instruction is an egregious error in theory and practice—the belief that competence can be constructed one bit at a time in quite arbitrary sequences. Analyze in detail all the things an expert can do (so the belief goes), and then teach these things one at a time to a beginner, and the beginner will become an expert. Readers know the alphabet, so teach the alphabet. They can do phonics, so teach phonics. They seem to know what you are talking about when you refer to letters, words, and sentences, so teach definitions of letters, words, and sentences. All of this overlooks how or why experts acquired their skills in the first place and ends up getting most things backwards. Reading makes you good at the alphabet, phonics, and all the rest. Membership in the literacy club makes all the skills available to children, but insistence on separate skills as prerequisites simply keeps children out of the club.

But the final, most potent and destructive reason for many of the programs imposed on teachers is *control*. It is a matter of power and lack of trust. Teachers need programs if they do not trust children to learn, if they fear that involvement in written language will not be sufficient to promote children's learning to read. People outside the classroom insist on programs if they do not trust teachers to teach, if they feel teachers must be controlled every step of the way.

SOME INSTRUCTIONAL ISSUES

A number of special issues frequently associated with reading instruction are not discussed at length in this book, partly because in the long run they are irrelevant to an analysis of reading. I am referring to such topics as dyslexia, learning disability, remedial reading, readiness, and dialect differences. These are certainly not issues that are irrelevant to reading *instruction*, because they can make a considerable difference to what a teacher does, or feels free to do, in the classroom. And regrettably these issues can make a considerable difference to the opportunities open to a child for learning to read. But these are not in my opinion matters that involve variations in the nature of reading among different people, or indeed in the way individuals best learn to read. There can be no doubt that some children find learning to read harder than others, but little reason to believe that they learn differently—that reading is a different kind of problem for them—and that therefore a difference in instructional approach is required.

Dyslexia

This term is a name, not an explanation. Dyslexia means, quite literally, being unable to read. Children who experience difficulty learning to read are frequently called dyslexic, but their difficulty does not arise because they *are* dyslexic or because they *have* dyslexia; they are dyslexic because they cannot read. To say that dyslexia is a cause of not being able to read is analogous to saying that lameness is a cause of not being able to walk. We were all dyslexic at one stage of our lives and become dyslexic again whenever we are confronted by something that we cannot read. The cure for dyslexia is to read.

It is a common belief, reflected in some dictionary definitions, that dyslexia is a medical condition resulting from a brain defect or malfunction. The origin of this belief is the incontrovertible medical fact that individuals once able to read may have their ability impaired as a consequence of damage to the brain from injury or illness, just as they may lose powers of speech or movement. Similarly a child with a damaged brain may have difficulty learning to read. But such children will manifest other difficulties too, and they constitute a very small proportion of all children indeed (very much smaller than the proportion of children who have difficulty learning to read). Brain-damaged children are not usually found in regular classrooms. And the fact that in rare cases of brain defect learning in general may be affected does not mean the converse—that a specific difficulty in learning to read indicates a brain defect. The latter view is so widespread that its rejection bears emphasis: *there is no convincing evidence that children who have difficulty learning to read but exhibit no other symptoms suffer from a brain defect or dysfunction.*

Obviously, children must be able to see and to understand language if they are to learn to read easily, but if these abilities are present there is no theoretical or medical reason why a child should fail to learn to read. No one has ever conducted a post mortem examination of the brain of a non-reading child and found a specific defect or disorder to which the handicap could be attributed. The notion that children can have a *specific learning disability* exclusive to reading as a consequence of brain malfunction is a myth. The term specific disability is again simply a label for an inadequately understood state of affairs, not an explanation. The learning disability is in fact *deduced* from the failure to read; the only evidence for the diagnosis is the very condition it is supposed to explain, rather like saying that fever is caused by having a high temperature. Because no specific brain defect or dysfunction causing inability to learn to read has ever in fact been observed, or even indicated by tests, the lack of physical evidence is sometimes accounted for by the assertion that the brain defect or dysfunction is "minimal." In place of an acknowledgment that there might be no defect at all, the "explanation" is offered that the defect is so small as to be undetectable.

There are no specific learning disabilities, in the sense that children who can see well enough to distinguish cars and animals and people might not see well enough to read, or that children who understand language well enough to comprehend speech might still not be able to read. Obviously, children who cannot see or comprehend speech will have difficulty learning to read, but they have visual or language problems generally, not specific reading disabilities.

As I have said before, there are many reasons why children who cope perfectly well with the world and school in every other respect might show little progress in learning to read, ranging from anxiety or disinterest to actually having the wrong idea of what reading is. Failure to learn to read does not require a medical explanation, and pseudo-medical explanations for children whose only impairment seems to be in learning to read are not only unjustified, they are dangerous. Children regarded as brain damaged are unlikely to be treated in the same way as children regarded as "normal." Teachers told that a child is dyslexic should always inquire into the symptoms of the disability, and if told that failure to read is the only symptom they should understand that they are not being told anything that they do not know already or could find out without a specialist's diagnosis. If told that the dyslexia is a consequence of brain damage they should ask how the handicap is manifested in other ways, and if told that the defect is minimal and restricted only to reading they should recognize that the diagnosis is based on a poor understanding of reading and a complete lack of supporting evidence.

Reversals

The tendency to give unnecessary and inaccurate medical explanations for quite normal kinds of behavior is well illustrated by the phenomenon of *reversals*—the apparent confusion of pairs of letters like *b* and *d* or *p* and *q*, and even pairs of words like *was* and *saw* or *no* and *on*. Misreadings of this kind are conspicuous in some children and may provoke "treatment" that can make learning to read more difficult. In fact, the discrimination of mirror-image figures is not easy, mistakes can be made by anyone, and the problem invariably goes away as the individual learns to read.

The discrimination of *b* from *d* is difficult because the difference between the two letters is minimal—a matter of whether the upright stroke is on the left or the right of the circle—and is not a difference that is significant or even relevant in most other aspects of our experience. A dog is a dog whether it is facing right or left; a car is a car whether it is traveling west or east. Only letters of the alphabet change their name depending on the direction they are facing. (Those more general discriminations that do require distinctions of actual or relative direction, such as "left" and "right" or telling the time from the hands of a clock, are notoriously difficult for most children.)

Not only is the *b*–*d* distinction difficult for children learning to read because of its unusual and minimal nature, it is also one of the easiest for adults to confuse. Of course we do not usually mistake *b* and *d* when we read, but that is primarily because we have so many other clues and are not looking at the letters in the first place. Fluent readers could make sense of print if every *b* were changed into *d* and vice versa, or if every *b* and *d* were obliterated altogether. But to distinguish *b* from *d* when the letters occur in isolation, one at a time, is much harder, and the fact that we can normally do so with facility must be attributed to the years of experience we have had and the amount of time we are given, relatively speaking, to inspect the evidence. Put a fluent reader in a situation where a minimum of visual information is available, for example by flashing the letter briefly on a screen, and there is a high probability that if a mistake is made at all it will be to confuse *b* with *d*, *p* with *q*.

Because the difference between *b* and *d* is both unusual and difficult to perceive, it is relatively difficult for children to learn, especially if they are not given adequate opportunity to observe and practice making the distinction, or if they are confused about the distinction in the first place. Children cannot "see" a difference if they do not understand what it is or the difference that it makes. It is completely nonsensical to say that reversals are caused by "seeing backwards." Seeing backwards is a logical and physical impossibility. It is physically impossible to see *part* of our field of view one way and the rest the other—to see two cars going one way and one the reverse direction when they are all in fact heading the same way. A child who sees a letter backwards would have to see everything else backwards at the same time, including the paper or board on which the letter was written. But it is logically impossible for *everything* to be seen backwards, because each element would still be seen in the same relationship with every other element, and paradoxically therefore everything would still appear to be the right way around.

Sometimes it is argued that children must be seeing letters backwards because they *write* them that way. But writing requires quite different kinds of skill altogether. We can all recognize faces and figures that we could not possibly reproduce accurately. If I try to draw a face and make it look like a potato, that does not mean that I see a face as a potato, it means that I am a poor artist. A child may draw a human figure as a circular head with matchstick arms and legs, but the picture does not indicate how the child sees a human figure. Show young children their own distorted drawings of a person and an artist's representation, and they will readily tell you which looks most like what they see. Children do not and cannot draw what they see, and the fact that they might write a few or many letters backwards says nothing about their vision, simply that they have not yet learned the difficult task of writing letters conventionally.

How should a child who makes reversals be treated? Confronted by the choice of helping children to circumvent a minor difficulty or of magnifying it into a major stumbling block, teachers may unwittingly act as if they have no choice at all and select the most difficult and least productive alternative. The importance of being able to distinguish *b* from *d* is grossly overrated. Skill in making the distinction is not required to become a reader, but becoming a reader makes distinguishing the two letters relatively simple, especially when they occur in meaningful print. When children have trouble with letters, perhaps confusing words like *big* and *dig*, it must be because they are reading words or sentences that are essentially meaningless (or as if they are meaningless). No one who is reading for sense could confuse words like *big* and *dig*, or *was* and *saw*, in a meaningful context.

But instead of being encouraged to use meaning to help unravel the confusion of similar looking words, children who encounter difficulty are likely to be given concentrated exercises requiring them to distinguish word pairs like *big* and *dig* in isolation; this is not only more difficult but is almost certainly going to increase apprehension and bewilderment. And if they show no progress with words in isolation the children may be restricted to drills with *b* and *d* alone. But letters in isolation are considerably more difficult than letters in words because an important clue has been removed. The difference between *b* and *d* at the beginning of a word is that the upright stroke is on the outside for *b* (as in *big*) but on the inside for *d* (as in *dig*). But "outside" and "inside" are meaningless for letters in isolation. There is only one possible way of making learning to distinguish *b* and *d* even more difficult, and that is to show the letters one at a time, so that there is no basis for comparison, expecting children to learn *b* before even meeting *d*. This, of course, is the logical final step of transforming the "problem" of reversal from a transient nuisance to complete consternation. The only treatment required to help a child avoid reversal errors is a solid regime of meaningful reading, so that a temporary difficulty is not magnified into an insurmountable handicap before the child learns to read.

Reading Readiness

The question of when a child becomes ready to begin learning to read is frequently asked. But it is asked more as a matter of administrative convenience or routine, inquiring whether a child is likely to show progress if given reading instruction, than to find out something meaningful about the child. Theoretically the question makes no sense at all. There is no magical day in a child's life, or degree of knowledge that a child must possess, when it can be said that the child passes from a state of being unable to learn to read to a state of being "ready." And there is certainly no test that will measure the state the child is in. There is no intellectual or linguistic basis for the notion of readiness. If learning to read is regarded as a continual process of making more and more sense of written language, advancing with every reading experience and beginning with the first insight that print is meaningful, then it will be seen that there can never be anything specific for a child to be ready for. Learning to read is simply a matter of reading more; children may at times be disinterested in further reading, but it does not make sense to say that for some physical or intellectual reason they are not *ready* to read more.

When the use of the term "reading readiness" in education is examined, it will be seen not to refer to readiness to read, nor even to readiness to learn to read, but to quite a different state of affairs, namely *readiness to cope with reading instruction*. Everything depends on the way in which children are expected to learn. If the instruction emphasizes knowledge of the alphabet, then children who cannot identify the letters will not be ready. If the instruction requires breaking spoken words down into imaginary sounds ("cat" is "kuh-a-tuh"), then children confused by this activity will not be ready. Every instructional procedure demands its price of admission, and children who cannot pay this price are not ready to make sense of the instruction. They certainly will not benefit from it. Reading and learning to read do not make exorbitant demands. Children need certain basic insights in order to develop as readers, but these insights come with reading (and with being read to) not by being deprived of reading experience. Reading demands visual acuity, but only the same acuity that a child uses in distinguishing familiar cars or animals or faces. Reading demands language ability, but it is the same ability that is demonstrated in comprehending a familiar form of speech. Reading demands the ability to learn, but any child who has made sense of a familiar world outside school has that ability. There is no question of *maturation* here, none of this is a matter of waiting until a child is physically ready. As far as vision is concerned, the eyes reach their optimum efficiency at the age of four; after that age senility begins to set in. The same applies to auditory acuity, with the added qualification that it is in any case not necessary to hear very well to learn to read because reading does not involve decoding to sound. All that is desirable is to be able to hear what the teacher is talking about.

Inventories exist that claim to catalog all the prerequisites for reading readiness. They are not usually informed by any kind of theory about the nature of reading, but are more like "shopping lists" of everything the compiler thinks might be relevant to reading, ranging from "knowledge of letters and sounds" to physical and emotional maturity and even "correct body-book posture" (as if a child with no experience of reading should be expected to hold a book intelligently). But as I have already discussed, while it is true that children who know the alphabet, and who are good at phonics, and who understand terms like "word" and "sentence," tend to be good readers, in each case the ability to read is a cause rather than a consequence of the particular skill. Obviously the child who is most ready to read is the child who can read already (not such a facetious suggestion, since it is only children who cannot read who are "not ready." Like the cure for dyslexia, readiness comes with reading.)

The reading problems that children have reflect the instruction they are expected to make sense of. Only children in phonics classes have "poor auditory memories" while reversals are only found in classes where meaningless visual discriminations are involved. Similarly, the age at which reading problems occur reflects the age at which children are expected to learn to read. In countries where formal instruction begins at the age of five, reading problems begin to appear among children aged six. Where formal efforts to teach reading begin at age eight, the onset of reading problems does not occur until age nine. Always the child with the reading problem, or who is not ready to read, is the one who cannot make sense of a particular instruction at the time it is offered.

One might think that children have to be at just the right age, and in the most favorable circumstances, if they are to succeed in learning to read. But the evidence is otherwise. Children need not be very "mature" to learn to read; many children of three and even two years of age have succeeded. But the children of two and three have other things to do than read, and few books are written that are of interest to two-year-olds. Besides, it is not necessary to be very young to learn to read. Illiterate peasants in the jungles of South America learn to read in less than two months, once their instructors have found a way to engage their interest and have provided material that is relevant to them. It is not necessary to be very "privileged" materially to learn to read, or to speak with a particular dialect; many poor children in all cultures have succeeded in solving the problem. It is not even necessary to be very smart to learn to read; indeed, it is being able to read that makes many people seem so smart. And it is certainly not necessary to have specialized programs and materials to learn to read.

The basic requirements are easily stated: on the part of the learner an interest in learning to read (or more precisely, in making sense of print) and for the teacher, the ability to find interesting print that the child can make sense of. In the latter respect, teachers can be just as "unready" as learners.

Once again I am not saying that all children will learn to read effortlessly at any age; obviously that is not the case. Lack of interest and lack of confidence will certainly interfere, as will evident physical defects like poor vision or mental retardation. It is also always possible that something will go wrong with the instruction. But none of these is a matter of "readiness" in an intellectual or physical sense; none will be solved by waiting until the child is older, or acquires another skill or two. Children should not all be expected to learn to read at the same time or at the same rate or from the same materials, for the simple reason that children are individuals. This individuality may be an administrative inconvenience, but it is one that education must try to capitalize on rather than eradicate. Children who cannot understand certain materials or activities from which they are expected to learn to read in school do not have a reading problem; the problem is the school's.

Children have reading problems when they read "below grade level," but grade levels have no reality outside the administrative organization of school; they certainly do not reflect any condition of the human brain. The fact that a nine-year-old reads like an average eight-year-old is not in itself cause for dismay. It does not mean that the child will never catch up. No one worries if an eight-year-old reads like an average eight-year-old; why should it matter if the child happens to be a year older? This matter of grade levels is purely a school concern. No one ever talks of a thirty-year-old reading like a twenty-nine-year-old, and we all read like a beginner when we are having difficulty reading.

Remedial Reading

Children are "ready" in reading instruction whenever they can engage in reading that makes sense to them, when they have joined the literacy club. Sometimes children seem to come to a dead end in learning to read, or to experience unusually severe difficulty in getting started. For such children it is frequently argued that a different approach is required. It may be safe to leave children who are not having difficulty to direct and control their own learning, but for others a more "structured" program is called for. "Problem readers" are often said to need exercises and drills before exposure to meaningful reading can be risked. But the reverse is the case. Phonics is a cumbersome and unreliable system for any child, but especially for children finding it hard to make sense of reading. The analysis of spelling-to-sound correspondences that I have given in this book is a statement about the nature of *language* itself, and cannot be thought to hold true for some people but not for others. And it would be perverse to argue that a strategy of reading that will not work for good readers should be especially appropriate for children who find difficulty with reading.

Children who find it hard to make sense of reading need more meaningful reading, not less. Drilling children in a few simple letter-sound correspondences may seem to help them make progress in learning, but this progress should always be weighed against the degree to which it may persuade children that reading is not in fact a meaningful activity. Paradoxically, children who do not learn to read easily are often expected to learn in the most difficult way possible. They may be assigned to remedial reading programs that are neither remedial nor reading. The most effective means of helping children of all ages who are in difficulty is to show them that reading is not a painful and pointless academic exercise and that learning to read is well within their grasp.

Dialect

Here is another source of individual difference that in principle should not have the slightest relevance for reading or learning to read, but which in fact often has considerable consequences for reading instruction. The whole notion that the dialect a person speaks is relevant to learning to read is based on the mistaken assumption that written language represents a particular spoken dialect.

As I discussed in Chapter 7, written language is not the same as anyone's spoken language, and probably for good reason. There is no reason to believe that it is necessary to speak a particular variety of spoken language in order to learn to read; on the contrary, written language should be easier for learning to read than attempts to imitate anyone's spoken dialect.

Part of the misunderstanding derives from a confusion between language production and comprehension. It is no more necessary to *speak* a certain dialect in order to be able to read than it is to speak the dialect in order to understand it when it is spoken. We can all understand dialects that we can speak only imperfectly at best. People from different geographical regions of a country may speak quite differently, but this does not prevent them from comprehending the same national magazines and the same television programs. One great advantage of written language is that it cuts across so many dialects. People can understand each other's writing when they would find each other's speech quite difficult. The spelling of written words is not an exact representation of the sounds of anyone's spoken dialect, just as no one talks in the sentence structures of written language. Written language has its own characteristics and conventions that are in principle accessible to speakers of any dialect.

A concomitant of the frequent confusion between the language we produce and the language we comprehend, incidentally, is an unfortunate tendency to evaluate children's language ability, and even their capacity to learn, on the language they produce. We can all understand language that we could not possibly produce (why otherwise would we bother to read books or listen to people talking?), and particular circumstances can always result in our being even more incoherent or tongue-tied than usual. The only fair way to assess an individual's ability to comprehend language is to examine the language that the individual does in fact comprehend.

It is particularly unfair to evaluate a child's ability to comprehend in reading by the way in which the child reads aloud. As I have tried to show in this book, reading aloud is always more difficult than reading silently because on top of the basic task of making sense of the text is the added problem of identifying and articulating each individual word correctly. A child who reads aloud "Johnny ain't got no candy" when the text is *Johnny hasn't any candy* is making sense of the print and reproducing it in a form that also makes sense. It might only serve to confuse such a child to insist that the reading should be word perfect. On the other hand another child who gets every word right may not have the slightest idea of the meaning for the simple reason that the child would not normally talk in that way.

But for many children in school, there is more to learning to read than making sense of print. There is also the matter of making sense of the instruction, and it is here that critical problems occur. A teacher who requires children to master a particular dialect in order to make sense of the instruction is obviously going to find problems among speakers of other dialects. So is a teacher who unconsciously or otherwise rejects a child's dialect, or suggests that the dialect is inferior or in some way inadequate for the child's learning to read. Teachers should be aware of their own dialect; distinctions they think they observe may not in fact be part of their speech. Most of us feel we pronounce *caught*, *court*, and *cot* as three distinct sequences of sounds when in fact we probably do not. We may think we are making sense, but if a child hears us saying "That word is not court, it is court," we are both likely to end up frustrated and confused.

Evidently, the extent to which teachers and pupils speak and comprehend different dialects is likely to have a bearing on how well the children will understand the instruction and how much they may become confused in learning to read. But the problem of dialect is minimized if reading is regarded as making sense of print, and emphasis on word-perfect oral reading is reduced.

Some readers may object "But shouldn't all children learn to speak good English?" (or "proper English," which usually means a particular dialect). Perhaps so—this is another debatable issue, but it is not a matter that should be allowed to interfere with learning to read. Trying to change the way a child speaks during reading instruction can only serve to add intellectual and emotional confusion, not to mention hostility toward the teacher and education in general.

It is not however uncommon for reading to be confused with something else (like spoken language competence) or for children to be expected to learn reading and something else at the same time. Mathematics or social science teachers, for example, may complain that children do not read well enough to comprehend their texts or tests, when in fact what the children lack is comprehension of the subject matter. Perhaps certain children are inadequate in both respects; they are poor readers and they are also confused in the particular subject area. But in that case the subject matter must be taught in some other way. Children will not advance in the subject area if they cannot read the text, and they will not improve in their reading if the subject matter is opaque to them. The only solution for the teacher is to try to ensure that both reading and the subject matter are made as easy as possible, which means keeping them separate for the child having difficulty with both.

Reading and Spelling

This is another case where the confusion of two quite distinct learning tasks can make both more difficult. Sometimes it is argued that if children are not taught to read by phonics, they will never learn to spell. But in the first place, knowledge of phonics is not much help for spelling. The spelling-to-sound correspondences that are so unreliable for decoding written words to sound are equally misleading for trying to move from the sounds of speech to correct spelling. Children who spell "by ear" are the worst spellers; spelling is basically a matter of convention with the best clues always being provided by meaning. Words that have similar meanings tend to be spelled alike. It is no use trying to employ phonic rules to work out how *medicine* (*medisin?*) and *medical* (*medikal?*) are spelled; they share the same root meaning and thus the same spelling pattern. In the long run, spellings must be remembered, although the more words we already know, the easier it is to spell and to remember new spellings. That does not mean that children should be taught spelling from word lists—the thousands of words that most of us can spell were learned not ten at a time from the word lists in our workbooks, but as a consequence of meaningful reading.

The second objection to the confusion of reading with spelling is that spelling has nothing to do with making reading possible (though reading can certainly facilitate learning to spell). We all know good readers who are poor spellers, and the more concentrated the reading, the less likely it is that attention will be paid to spelling. As I showed in earlier chapters of this book, we do not normally look at letters as we read; we read directly for meaning. If we do deliberately attend to spelling then we probably are having difficulty with what we read and employing an inefficient strategy to overcome that difficulty. I certainly do not want to suggest that children should not learn to spell correctly. On the contrary, it is by keeping reading and spelling instruction clearly separate that children get the best opportunities to develop proficiency in both. I am not saying that children cannot apply themselves to learn quite unrelated skills concurrently; they can begin to learn to read and write at the same period of their lives just as they begin learning to speak and comprehend spoken language at the same time. Learning about spoken language is not complete nor does it have to stop when children's attention is turned to print. Learning about all aspects of language can be mutually supportive, although children will find not being permitted to concentrate on one particular aspect at one particular time bewildering. The choice must be left to the child. It is not necessary for teachers to feed instruction to children one bit at a time, but they have to be careful that children do not become confused or anxious because of temporarily inappropriate feedback. To make any aspect of language learning an issue—spelling, oral expression, written expression, neatness, even speed—when the child's concern is with a different aspect will disrupt both the teacher's and the child's intentions.

THE CHALLENGE OF TEACHING READING

The analysis of reading contained in this book cannot immediately change the world for teachers. I do not expect that many teachers will find it easy or even practicable to put new insights that they have gained into practice. Teachers may have few choices about what they actually do in class; they may be locked into a limited range of programs and procedures. They may work in unsuitable classrooms with too many children in competitive, anxious, and even hostile atmospheres. A frequent need to test, evaluate, and show "accountability" can induce tension and fear of failure in teacher and child alike.

Teachers may find it difficult to change what they do for all kinds of reasons—pressure from parents, the expectations of their superiors, the resistance of colleagues threatened by any suggestion of change or improvement, the sheer inertia of tradition in education, and the dead weight of their own training and the daily rituals and frustration in the classroom. The idea that learning should be made easy for children, rather than "challenging" (a synonym for "difficult"), can offend an ingrained puritanism in many teachers—which infects children and parents—while a class in which everyone is happily reading something of personal interest may be criticized as a place where no "work" is being done. Teachers can lack the time to think about fundamental change or lack moral support to go through with it. An inescapable consideration is that most children are not angels—they do not settle down to learn (what teachers want) in the cooperative way that may seem to be implied in the discussions of this book or that is taken for granted by many formal programs. Children can be aggressive, apathetic, distracted, or just downright cussed for reasons that no amount of learning or understanding on the part of teachers can do very much about. All of these constitute problems for *reading instruction,* but they do not change the nature of reading or the way in which it must be learned.

Despite all the limitations upon what teachers can do, they are still better off knowing more about what facilitates learning to read and what interferes with it. A new understanding will not directly change the world for teachers, but it can provide them with confidence to try to bring some changes about or simply to buck the trend. Understanding why certain conditions or activities make both learning and teaching more difficult can relieve the anxiety and minimize the consequences for teachers and children alike, particularly in terms of their self-respect.

Ultimately, teachers of reading may find they have to do most of their educating *outside* the classroom, teaching parents, administrators, and politicians the real way that children learn to read, and showing them that they, the teachers, know best. Because the fundamental issue with programs is often control, the teachers' response may have to be political. They may have to assert their need, responsibility, and ability to be in charge of what they do in their own classrooms. That is the challenge of teaching reading.

Summary

The primary concern of teachers must be to ensure that all children are admitted into the literacy club, where they can see written language employed in a variety of useful and meaningful ways and can receive assistance in employing written language themselves. Accuracy and "skills" should not be stressed at the expense of meaningfulness to the child; they are a consequence rather than a prerequisite of reading experience. Teachers must protect themselves and their students from effects of programs and tests, which can persuade children that reading is nonsensical, painful, and pointless.

Dyslexia is not a medical condition, seeing backwards is a physical impossibility, and "readiness" for reading is a mythical barrier.

9

Enter the Computer

Whether teachers want it or not, the world of education is changing rapidly. The personal computer has entered the scene. Computers are already a part of most schools, if not of most classrooms. Parents and other groups are buying computers to be put into all classrooms. They are urging schools to move into the computer age. Many educational planners are *insisting* that schools move into the computer age. The advance of computers will not be stopped if teachers turn their backs on them. More likely computers will take over while teachers are not looking. Teachers will not be able to barricade their classrooms against computers, but they should not surrender to them either. Every teacher must understand computers.

Emotional objections that electronic devices can never replace teachers will have little effect. Many influential people, including computer and educational programmers, software developers, publishers, politicians, trustees, and administrators, already believe that computers are cheaper than teachers. And computers *are* cheaper—for those things they are able to teach. They also believe that computers are more efficient than teachers; this is true for those things that computers teach best. The question is not whether computers should be allowed into classrooms, but how they will be used. The question is still one of who is to be in charge—the question I said was critical as far as programmatic instruction was concerned—except now it is much more acute. Teachers could lose more than their authority; they could lose their vocation.

Computers can do very little directly to help children learn to read. The kind of systematic instruction that computers are currently most suited to, and that in the minds of those who promote programs is the ideal way to teach reading, will do the most damage to literacy. On the other hand, computers indirectly can do a great deal of good for literacy development generally, expanding the world of written language and facilitating the entry of newcomers into it. There is much

154

that is positive to be said about computers, but I propose to deal with the negative side first. The perils are the most immediate.

The Ultimate Programming Machine

It is as drill-and-test devices—sometimes euphemistically referred to as teaching machines—that computers today are widely seen as most relevant to education. Not only are they capable of presenting the most trivial, decontextualized, and fragmented drills in endless variation, but they do so with an extreme degree of efficiency, with impeccable record keeping, and in a manner highly attractive to both students and teachers.

Uncertain or apprehensive teachers are generally willing to hand over the task of constructing educational programs to experienced software developers. Some will not take the computer into their classrooms unless the software is guaranteed. But the repetitive presentation of isolated items for the student to learn by rote, followed by simple questions where the responses can be checked against "correct answers" and the results scored and stored for future reference, is in fact the easiest kind of computer program to write. Every bit of nonsensical activity ever put on paper can be reproduced in software, and in living color as well, by "experts" with little or no classroom competence or experience.

Educators themselves do not necessarily demonstrate greater sophistication when it comes to programming computers for literacy instruction. I have heard committees of teachers, linguists, and other language-education authorities at reading conferences discuss how computer-based "instructional modules" might be created. Much of the time they talked of what they thought the computer could most conveniently do, not of what would make sense or be of value to the learner. They talked of repetitive tasks with right and wrong answers, the correction of "mistakes," tests, scores, and the keeping of records, all the grist of mechanical programmatic instruction, all totally unrelated to the way written language is actually used and learned outside the classroom.

They talked frequently and even cheerfully about language that would be distorted in some way, of sentences and paragraphs containing blanks that the learner would be required to fill in, or with extraneous words for the learner to detect and remove, even of totally random arrangements of words that the computer would obligingly generate for the learner to try to reorganize. All of this was highly ingenious in conception and application, and all of it was completely artificial. No one in real life ever leaves blanks in written sentences for the reader to fill in, or adds superfluous words to try to catch the reader out. No one ever speaks or writes nonsense to anyone else, except as part of something that is clearly recognizable as a game, not as a "learning activity."

I do not think that the experts at these literacy conferences were deliberately planning to teach children that written language was essentially nonsense. I do not think they were thinking of written language or of children at all, but of what the computer could do.

It is all so compelling. I have seen groups of teachers crowding around the software displays that are beginning to outnumber book displays at reading conferences. One I remember that attracted a particularly large crowd had a segment in which a large cartoon rabbit with floppy ears was depicted in dazzling rainbow colors. Alongside were the letters R—BBIT. The task, of course, was to fill in the blank. The demonstrator urged members of the crowd to try incorrect letters first. When someone put in a K, the rabbit's ears drooped, buzzers sounded, and a mournful voice invited another attempt. When the right letter was finally offered, bells rang, lights flashed, the ears perked up, and the rabbit got a carrot. What struck me particularly was the evident rapture on the face of the demonstrator, who must have seen this segment hundreds of times—and was still enthralled. The segment was part of an "integrated" program that claimed to take care of all aspects of reading instruction; it comprised scores of disks and cost thousands of dollars. Technically the production was superb. Visually it was seductive. What will it teach children about reading?

For anyone who thinks that learning will take place only if it is continually monitored and measured, who believes that anything a drill can teach must be important, especially if it is packaged and promoted under an imposing label (such as "comprehension skills" or "total reading"), then computer-based instructional programs are enormously attractive. It is not difficult to sell them to some administrators on the basis of their record-keeping capabilities alone, or to impress unsuspecting teachers and children with their presumed importance and value. One commercial reading program actually boasts that it can get children to attend to material that would be too boring to present any other way. The nature and purposes of written language seem in danger of being forgotten completely.

The negative side of computers in literacy education is that children, parents, and teachers will become persuaded that these nonsensical and pointless activities are what constitute reading and teaching reading. For children who are already learning to read—to make sense of written language—the danger is that exposure to such programs will persuade them that they were wrong about reading. Children learn from what is demonstrated to them. For children who have difficulties with reading the risks are even greater. They will be required to spend even more time on the nonsense, and will have even less chance of ever joining the literacy club.

Incidentally, there is obviously not much of a place for teachers when computers are allowed to take over in this way. Children very quickly learn to put the instructional disk into the drive and the computer tells them what should be done next.

Computers in the Literacy Club

Computers offer a number of indirect advantages to teachers of reading—when they (the computers and the teachers) are not being used as teaching machines. A computer can help put children in touch with what they might want to read; it can tell them where to find particular books, magazines, and newspapers that they might desire or find interesting and useful; and it can present on its own screen "information" that they might find relevant to a purpose of their own. Computers can also stimulate reading on their own account. Children interact with the words that appear on the screen as they use a computer, they consult the manuals (especially if they happen to be written in language that children can understand), and they can be inspired to read books about computers and the kinds of things computers can do. For children, computers can be interesting things to work on and to think, talk, read, and write about, even when the children's particular interests are as diverse as art, music, science, or sports.

But it is as a tool for writing that computers can most help reading. As I said earlier, despite the topic focus of this book, it is impossible to treat reading and writing separately, whether in theory or in practice. At this point I must talk about what computers can do for writers—and for children learning to write—to show how computers can truly enhance the possibilities for children in the literacy club, helping them attain fluency in both writing and reading.

It is widely known how useful computers can be to anyone who writes when they are used as word processors, with a small printer. Word processors combine the ease and speed of an electric typewriter with the flexibility of pencil and paper. There is no easier way to get ideas into written language, to erase, revise, move things around, edit, store, and recover. Few professional writers reject word processors once they get to know them, even though they may have used (or refused to use) electric typewriters for years. Anything that makes the act of writing easier makes learning to write easier.

There are other advantages of word processors not so commonly understood, for example in checking spelling and suggesting vocabulary. There is no longer any need to worry about the spelling of those awkward words that always defeat us, or to interrupt the flow of thought while we consult a dictionary. Just put down anything, even an initial letter, and the computer will sort it all out against its own spelling list when the composition is done. There is no need to go to the thesaurus for that word that is so irritatingly on the tip of your tongue. A touch of the key can provide you with a set of synonyms (or antonyms) for any notion you have in mind.

Some teachers will object to these time- and labor-saving facilities for the same reason that there have been doubts about the use of electric typewriters and arithmetical calculators in classrooms—that they may make attention to basic skills unnecessary and therefore interfere with learning. But it is a mistake to believe that obstacles are the most efficacious motivators; there is no evidence that making an activity artificially difficult facilitates learning. Quite the reverse, lack of knowledge of spelling and vocabulary reduces the amount of writing that is done, especially when mistakes are penalized. A comfortable facility with reading and writing, on the other hand, makes learning the "basics" both continual and effortless.

Word processing computers can take care of two of the greatest concerns of beginning and fluent writers alike: legibility and speed. Readability is always a problem for writers, especially inexperienced young ones, even if not at the fetish level that neatness occasionally reaches in classrooms. One touch of a computer key and anyone has a perfectly formed letter that can be printed in a compact and properly aligned orientation. No need even to remember that in English print goes from left to right, from top to bottom.

Computers help everyone to write—authors and secretaries, experienced practitioners and beginners. And what helps writing does more than involve reading; it helps and promotes reading. I have not just been talking about the composition of books or of complicated letters and term papers. I have in mind all the literacy club activities that can and should provide the opportunities for learning in any classroom concerned with reading and writing—with letters, labels, lists, notes, memoranda, newspapers, magazines, reviews, digests, advertisements, plans, schedules, recipes, and timetables, with every thread of the fabric of living language.

There is another advantage that computers have brought to writing, the most dramatic development to my mind that has occurred in language technology since it became possible for individuals to write at all. Computers are frequently and mistakenly believed to be solitary devices, isolating people from each other. But computers have, for the first time, made it possible for two or more people to write the same text together.

There is no longer need for a collaborator to lean over a child's shoulder. No need to take a draft away in order to read and comment upon it. I can show you what I am writing simply by reproducing my screen on your screen with the touch of a key. I can disclose to you all the contents of my memory (in computer terms at least). You can comment on what I have written, even propose changes, without interfering with me or offending me in any way. I can consider your suggestions as you make them, on my screen. If your changes please me, I can accept them, and if they do not, my original text will not be blemished.

No need any longer for a teacher painstakingly to instruct a child on the West Coast how to write a letter to a friend on the East Coast, or how to read the reply. West and East Coast children can write and read the letter together, simultaneously.

We shall all be closer in the future through computers, if we wish to be. Readers will be closer to authors, writers to editors, learners to practitioners. You may not have to wait for your favorite author's next novel to be published. If the author agrees you will be able to read it as it is being written, vicariously sharing the excitement and frustration of composition, the discipline of revision and editing. Imagine children being able to interact with their favorite authors in that way.

Imagine a living poem in every classroom. Every day teacher and children will be able to see how it has grown from the day before. Everyone will be able to add a branch or a flower—or to take a shoot away to grow a poem of their own. Why use computers to engage children in pointless ritual, when a fantastic world of written language possibilities is opening up in which everyone can participate? Instead of drill, computers can speed and facilitate the creative use of written language throughout the school day.

Learning About Computers

It may be suggested that I am now proposing a further obstacle for children on the way to becoming readers, requiring them to become proficient with computers before they are admitted to the world of reading. But children can learn about computers as they learn to read and to write, in exactly the same way that they learn to read and to write. They do not need courses in computer literacy, nor lessons in programming. All they need is people to help them do what they want to do. They need admission to the club of computer users. And the best guides, often, will be other children. Adults, not children, find computers complicated and intimidating.

I have been following the progress of a two-year-old child who has been mastering a computer almost as quickly as he has been mastering spoken language. He very quickly grasped how the machine was switched on, the use of "menus," and the need for particular disks to be inserted in the drive (which he asked his parents to do for him because his own fingers were still too clumsy). For months he has experimented with strings of letters that he will produce and erase according to schemes of his own, using the keyboard and screen as a scratchpad to experiment upon. Recently, without instruction, he typed his first words. These were not his name, or that of any member of his family. To the surprise of his parents, they discovered that he was typing LOAD and RUN, the two key words for getting the computer to do what he wanted.

Teachers must also learn about computers. If they do not understand them, or are afraid of them, then the programmers will take over. Once again, there is no need for a teacher to go off and take a course on computer literacy at the nearest college. Cramming the history of computers and the intricacies of Boolean algebra are enterprises that are useful and fascinating only to people who are already established members of the computer club. It is also not necessary to learn to program, a cabalistic skill that defeats many beginners with its obscure rituals and uncertain purposes. Even many instructional manuals should be avoided at the outset, since they appear to be written primarily for the benefit of people who already know what the authors are talking about.

The best way for teachers to learn about computers is the same as the best way for children—by using them with the help of some nonevaluative collaborator who is already a member of the club. For teachers, this collaborator will often be a child. In most schools and classrooms where computers have been installed, children are the experts. Children are the learners with the fewest apprehensions and preconceptions.

Learning about computers can be as exciting and productive for teacher and child as learning about reading should be. Computers need not destroy literacy, and they should not be allowed to destroy it. Who will be in charge—programmers and administrators outside the class-room, or teachers and children in the classroom, as members of the literacy club?

Summary

Computers make the conflict between teachers and programs for control of classrooms more acute. If computers are used simply to deliver programmatic instruction to children, they could destroy liter-acy by removing learning to read completely from the domain of utility and meaningfulness. But computers can be used by children as tools to assist them in their efforts to exploit the possibilities of written lan-guage. Electronic technology cannot be ignored in the classroom, and teachers must not leave decisions about how computers should be employed to outsiders.

For Further Reading

Details and more complete discussion of the research that underlies *Reading Without Nonsense* can be found in

Smith, Frank. *Understanding Reading.* 3d ed. New York: Holt, Rinehart and Winston, 1982.

A representative range of more specific articles on recent research in reading is in

Anderson, Richard A., Jean Osborn, and Robert J. Tierney, eds. *Learning to Read in American Schools.* Hillsdale, N.J.: Erlbaum, 1984.

A sensitive and interesting discussion of children's development in both reading and writing is

Harste, Jerome C., Virginia A. Woodward, and Carolyn L. Burke. *Language Stories and Literacy Lessons.* Portsmouth, N.H.: Heinemann Educational Books, 1984.

On the discouragements as well as the successes of bringing older children to literacy, see

Meek, Margaret. *Achieving Literacy.* Oxford: Oxford University Press, 1984.

My own analysis of writing is contained in

Smith, Frank. *Writing and the Writer.* New York: Holt, Rinehart and Winston, 1982.

A collection of outstanding papers on how young children in many different cultures make sense of written language, seen through the eyes of sociologists and anthropologists as well as linguists, psychologists, and teachers, is

Goelman, Hillel, Antoinette A. Oberg, and Frank Smith. *Awakening to Literacy.* Exeter, N.H.: Heinemann Educational Books, 1984.

Finally, a more discursive collation of my views on literacy and schools can be found in

Smith, Frank. *Essays Into Literacy*. Exeter, N.H.: Heinemann Educational Books, 1983.

Index